The Village
The Church
and
The Pub

A catalogue record of this book is available from the British Library
First Edition: April 2004
Second Edition: January 2005

ISBN: 0-9549455-0-6

Printed in England by Aspect Design, Malvern
www.aspect-design.net

Published by: Millar's Village Trails
Worcester Road, Malvern
Worcestershire WR14 1EX
Email: millarroy345@aol.com
Email: andrew.miller2@btinternet.com

The Village
The Church
and The Pub

*A tour of the North Cotswolds
and places in the neighbouring counties of
Worcestershire and Herefordshire*

by

Roy Millar

Millar's Village Trails

Dedication

*This book is dedicated to the memory of my brother Brian
and to my wife Barbara's sisters Joyce, Olive, Alice and Brenda
who with the exception of Joyce all had cancer.*

*The net profits from the sale of this book are being given
to the Cobalt Unit Appeal Fund at Cheltenham, the fund
serves Gloucestershire, Worcestershire and Herefordshire
in the fight against cancer.*

Contents

Chapter 7

Chapter 8

Chapter 9

Chapter 10

Chapter 11

Foreword

The Cotswolds and nearby villages of Worcestershire and Herefordshire are blessed with many beautiful churches, with surroundings that are unsurpassed. In compiling the information given in the following chapters, I have met many interesting people, as I do more often than not when visiting churches.

The villages and churches of these areas reflect much of the history of our country, old customs and laws such as burials in wool. To bury someone in anything other than wool was a punishable offence. The reason for this was that wool was the source of wealth for the area. Many of the tombs in the churchyards are in fact listed buildings. Some villages show much evidence of the Plague, the Civil War, the War of the Roses and the Reformation.

I have toured these counties for some 50 years and during the past 10 years I have visited over 1000 churches in England and Wales. I would like to express thanks to the churches for the mine of information provided. All sorts of literature is available and assists church funds. Many churches have recipe books and other souvenirs on sale. Pub licensees have also provided valuable information, giving historical details about their premises.

This guide is illustrated by Evesham artist Barbara Butcher, whose work is known to many for her landscape and floral paintings. I am grateful to her for her contribution and support.

My thanks also to my wife Barbara for her assistance and the patience which she has shown over the period I have spent visiting the various places, sometimes on several occasions in one week.

It is my hope that readers will visit the villages mentioned and that they will derive much pleasure in the tranquillity of the places described.

Roy Millar

Part 1

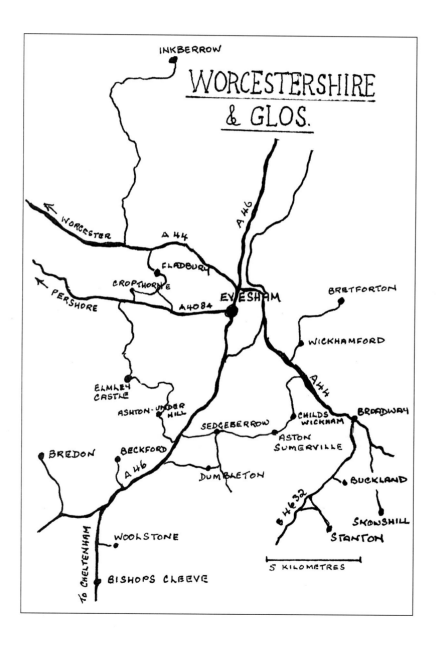

Chapter 1

Snowshill - Gloucestershire

◆ ◆ ◆

Buckland - Gloucestershire

◆ ◆ ◆

Stanton - Gloucestershire

The Village
SNOWSHILL . GLOUCESTERSHIRE
situated 2½ miles SW of Broadway

This small village has an idyllic setting and is well known for its natural beauty and remarkable views.

Snowshill Manor, which was the home of the late Sir Charles Wade, is a very important feature of the village. It is now owned by the National Trust and houses a huge collection of items amassed by Sir Charles during most of his lifetime. These items include musical instruments, toys, and a comprehensive collection of Samurai armour. The gardens attached to the Manor are a pleasure to visit.

The village was chosen to be one of the settings for the film 'Bridget Jones's Dairy' which starred Hugh Grant and Colin Firth. During the making of the film, which was in mid summer, 12 tonnes of artificial snow was deposited in the churchyard to create a winter scene.

On the edge of the village there is a lavender farm with a gift shop. Refreshments are available in the coffee shop on site. The farm is signposted in the village.

The Church
ST BARNABAS

This Victorian church is built of Cotswold stone and because of this, gives the appearance of having been built at an earlier date. It was actually built in 1864 on the same site as the Norman church.

Rectors can be traced back to 1269 and tithes to 1183. It is uncertain what happened to the previous church.

The windows are of Victorian stained glass. The font is 15th century and the pulpit is Jacobean c1640. In the churchyard there is a 17th century tomb with a typical inscription of the times.

The Pub
THE SNOWSHILL ARMS

Opposite the church and a very popular venue for visitors. Bar snacks are available.

♦ ♦ ♦

The Village
BUCKLAND . GLOUCESTERSHIRE
situated 1½ miles SW of Broadway
off Broadway-Winchcombe road

This pretty village is at the end of a no-through road. There is however a bridleway to Snowshill, so it is popular with hill walkers. The Manor House, once occupied by James Thynne, Lord of the Manor, is now a hotel. The Parsonage dates back to the 15th century and is one of the oldest in the country.

Ancient Cross - Buckland Church, Buckland

The Church
ST MICHAEL'S

Serves the parish of Buckland with Laverton and was a favourite of William Morris.

Upon entering the churchyard visitors are confronted by a restored 14th century preaching cross. No doubt this was where John Wesley delivered his orations when he visited Buckland, as well as from the pulpit. It was also where a market was held on its steps and local produce sold.

The church itself has origins dating from the 13th century. There have been several restorations, but these have not destroyed the beauty of the church. Its tower has demons as gargoyles and contains a peal of six bells. There is a clock and a chime mechanism. The latter was restored in 1997 and plays 'We love the place of God'.

Entering the church through the north porch into the north aisle, the Buckland Cope is on display in a showcase and is to the left. The expert needlecraft of the 15th century is a joy to see. It is believed to have come from the nearby Hailes Abbey. Also near the door is a stoup which was used for holy water.

The font is of the 15th century and has ornate carving. In the west of the church there is a 17th century oak gallery. The west door was used by shepherds to enter the church when they attended services with their dogs, as was the custom. They were seated in the pews in the south aisle. On display in this aisle is the 16th century mazer, a bowl made of maple wood. This was thought to have been used as a chalice until the 17th century and was replaced by a new chalice, which is still in use today. The parish chest can also be seen. This large chest is made of oak and is bound with iron. The floor tiles in the south aisle are dated as being 15th century, and were probably made by the Malvern Priory.

The aumbry which would have been used to house the altar plate is situated to the right of the chancel arch. The east window has three panels of painted glass. They may have originated from Hailes Abbey and were restored in the late 19th century by workmen under the supervision and direction of William Morris. The monument in the south wall of the chancel is a memorial to

James Thynne. The pulpit, pews and wainscoting are of the early 17th century.

The Pub

There is no pub in the village, the nearest being at Broadway or Stanton, which are equidistant. At Broadway there is a choice of several, one of the nearest being the **Crown and Trumpet Inn**, Church Street. This inn is situated just behind the village green. It is of the 17th century and is built of Cotswold stone. Its beamed and timbered bar and high backed settles make it an attraction to many visitors. The one time stables at the rear are believed to have been used to stable horses for assisting carters and carriers, as extra horses for pulling loads up the nearby Fish Hill.

◆ ◆ ◆

The Village
STANTON . GLOUCESTERSHIRE
situated 3 miles SW of Broadway
¼ mile off Broadway-Winchcombe road (B4352)

The village is typical of the Cotswolds with its houses built of the mellow Cotswold stone. The ancient village cross must be one of the most photographed scenes and a subject for many artists.

The Church
ST MICHAEL AND ALL ANGELS

Stands on a site of Saxon origins. It is believed that the church in those times was serviced by the monks of Winchcombe Abbey. Most records of this were destroyed in 1151 during a serious abbey fire.

In St Michael's there are three Norman pillars which form the north arcade of the nave. The south arcade was rebuilt in the early English style, after the central tower collapsed. There are fragments of mediaeval glass in the west window and south transept, also the east window. The pulpit dates back to 1684 and the lectern to 1375.

In the north transept there are frescoes of the Annunciation and Purification, fragments of panelling from the mediaeval screen, a passage squint and an aumbry. In the south transept and aisle another squint is to be seen. This, however, is not a full passage squint.

There are steps to the mediaeval screen and fragments of painted decoration, a further two aumbries, a piscina and traces of 15th century glass in the south window. Low down on the south wall are the remains of stone benches. These date back to the times when only the infirm and the aged used seating. It was usual for the people to stand. The expression 'the weakest to the wall' has its origins here.

The west window is 15th century and has a double transom. The piece of old glass is dated to about 1480 and shows the White Rose of York. At the back of the nave, mediaeval benching bears the scars of dog chains. Sheepdogs were brought to church by their masters, as was the custom of the time.

The rood screen and stone cross in the churchyard are by Sir Ninian Comper and commemorate the casualties of the 1914-1918 War. The font is of 15th century origins and the six bells are dated 1640. In the porch there are the remains of a holy water stoup. The steeple is perpendicular.

John and Charles Wesley made many visits to Stanton.

The Pub
THE MOUNT INN

Is reached by following the road straight up the village. The Mount provides excellent views over Stanton and the vale. It was built in the early 17th century and was occupied firstly as a private dwelling, after which it became an off-licence, and it was during this period that locals were known to hang a dartboard on a nearby tree to play darts and to obtain refreshments from the off-licence. It then came to its present form of usage. It has sporting connections with the village, cricket, rugby and football. It is a popular venue for hill walkers and visitors from abroad. Bar snacks are availiable.

♦ ♦ ♦

Chapter 2

Sedgeberrow - Worcestershire

◆ ◆ ◆

Dumbleton - Gloucestershire

◆ ◆ ◆

Childswickham - Worcestershire

◆ ◆ ◆

Aston Somerville
— Worcestershire

The Village
SEDGEBERROW . WORCESTSHIRE
situated off A46 Evesham-Cheltenham road
3 miles SW of Evesham
signposted off A46 onto B4078 leading into village

Although the village has Anglo-Saxon origins it now mainly consists of modern properties. However, in the heart of the village and intermingled with the modern housing there are some fine examples of timber frame and 17th/18th century houses to be seen.

Among the amenities of Sedgeberrow there is a village shop/post office that serves the community and there is a school. A play group provides for the younger ages. On the social side there is a Women's Institute group, a badminton club and a British Legion club, although there is no clubhouse.

The River Isbourn flows through the village and unusually flows north. There was once a water mill used for grinding flour, which closed shortly after the end of the Second World War.

Double Sedilia - St Mary The Virgin, Sedgeberrow

The Church
ST MARY THE VIRGIN

Is of Saxon origin but little trace of the Saxon church remains. The present church was consecrated on 16 September 1331. Built of blocks faced with Cotswold stone, it has had considerable restoration in Victorian times by William Butterfield, architect.

At the western end of St Mary's there is a hexagonal turret capped by an octagonal spire. This houses three bells. The building is in the transitional style from decorated to perpendicular. It consists of a chancel, nave, north porch and vestry.

Entry into the church is through the north door. The porch is almost certainly of the 14th century and within it lie the remains of a stoup which would once have held holy water. The church is open plan, the chancel and the nave being separated by a high oak screen. This was rebuilt by Butterfield.

In the north side of the chancel one of the windows contains a piece of 14th century stained glass. This shows a priest seated. In his left hand he holds a model of a church and in his right hand he holds two keys. The model of the church is not Sedgeberrow, as it shows a central steeple. It is probably symbolic and it is likely that the priest portrayed is St Peter.

The east window is of the 14th century and the glass is dated 1878. The window depicts Christ flanked by four biblical prophets, with these being flanked by angels. The reredos behind the altar is of the 14th century, but was rebuilt by Butterfield. This consists of three moulded stone compartments set into the wall. On the south wall of the sanctuary there is a canopied piscina with shelf. Next to this can be seen a double sedilia. This was for the priest and his assistant.

When the church was consecrated in 1331 three altars were dedicated, one of which is in the sanctuary, the other two were almost certainly in the nave. Evidence of one of these is the small niche in the south wall.

The floor tiles date from the restoration by Butterfield, as do the pulpit and the pews. The font is of the latter part of the 12th century. It is circular and plain, its cover being of a later date. The restorations carried out by William Butterfield were paid for in total by Mrs Barber, the widow of a former rector.

The Pub
QUEENS HEAD

A one time coaching inn built circa 1800. It retains some of its original features externally, but inside having undergone many refurbishments, little of its long past remains. Bar snacks and a full menu are available.

Ancient stone carving - Sedgeberrow

The Village
DUMBLETON . GLOUCESTERSHIRE
follow A46 Evesham-Tewkesbury
turn on to B4078 approx 4 miles south of Evesham
signposted to Dumbleton

The village consists of many 16th/17th century houses and is regarded as being an 'estate village'. It has a village shop which provides for many of the villagers' needs. The village hall is over 100 years old and also serves as a kindergarten. There is a village cricket team, who have recently had a new cricket pavilion erected.

Dumbleton Hall was the home of the Cocks family and their estate occupied much of the surrounding land. The Hall was built about 1534 and was in their possession for over 200 years. When Sir Richard Cocks died in the latter part of the 18th century, the Hall fell into disrepair and was demolished.

The present Hall was built in the mid 19th century on a different site within the grounds, using Cotswold stone. It became the home of the Eyres family in 1930. The Eyres family were popular hosts with their house parties. They entertained many prominent members of society, including John Betjeman (poet laureate) and the Mitford sisters.

In 1959 the Hall became a hotel and was used by the post office as a low cost holiday venue for employees in need of convalescence. Now the hotel is no longer connected with the post office and is completely independent. It is a venue for conferences, as well as other functions and holidays.

There is an annual village fête.

The Church
ST PETER'S

This Norman church is built of stone and occupies the site of an earlier Saxon church which would have almost certainly been constructed of wood. It has a western tower added on in the 13th century with further alterations in the 15th century, when the embattlements were added.

The tower houses six bells, all dated 1729 and re-hung in 1892.

All were made by Abraham Rudhall II of Gloucester. The clock was installed in 1830.

Entry to the church is via the north door, over which a carved tympanum can be seen. This is the mask of an animal that has foliage coming from its mouth. Many such carvings can be seen on churches of the period.

Major alterations were carried out in the 14th century when a transept was built on the north side. The northern half of this transept was later partitioned off, to be used as a vestry.

The north and west windows are in the decorated style 1300-1350AD. The chancel arch and south west window of the nave is of around the same date. In the south wall of the chancel there are two piscinas. One is of the 13th century and the other originates from the 14th century.

The painted monument is of Sir Charles Percy, who was the son of the Earl of Northumberland. The seating and pulpit were donated by the Eyres family in 1905. The font was made in 1661 in the style of the 14th century.

The Pub

There is no pub in Dumbleton, but just a short distance away in the village of Sedgeberrow is **The Queen's Head**.

Church archway - St Peters

The Village
CHILDSWICKHAM . WORCESTERSHIRE
a short distance from Broadway
travel along B4632 Broadway-Winchcombe road
approx 1½ miles along this road Childswickham is signposted

Childswickham was at one time part of the county of Gloucestershire. This was altered when a transfer order came into force 1 April 1931. It is surrounded by market gardening land and farms. Evidence of a moat around the village can still be found.

In the centre of the village there is the base and column of an ancient cross. The cross itself has been replaced by an 18th century urn, as the cross had eroded to the point of disintegration. It was a preaching cross and was where the priest would deliver his messages of the Gospel. It is situated on what was probably in those times the main road from London to Worcester. It was also a place where a market would be held.

The Church
ST MARY'S

St Mary's was almost certainly built on the site of a previous church. It would have been constructed of wood with origins of about the 8th or 9th century. The church now is constructed of stone and consists of a chancel, nave, and north transept, with embattled western tower complete with pinnacles and spire, containing six bells. The tower and spire are of the 15th century. There was formerly a south transept. The old nave and transept was believed to have been built in the 12th century.

The church was rebuilt in 1870 at a cost of £1,100. In 1874 further works were carried out and a new chancel was built at a cost of £600. As with many Victorian restorations, the interior displays little of its original appearance. All that remains is window tracery, two pillars and two niches. The niches are situated in the north and south walls of the nave. It will be observed that the mediaeval craftsmen had a sense of humour when carving the faces therein. The niches now house modern carved figures, which depict Jesus as a child in Mary's arms and the Apostle St John.

Mary & Child - St Peters

The stained glass window near the statue of St John is modern and was donated by the villagers to commemorate the Silver Jubilee of Queen Elizabeth II. It can be seen that the window features the church tower and the mediaeval village cross. The two pillars stand against the north and south walls of the chancel. The window in the south wall of the chancel is mediaeval and has been copied into the windows of the nave installed in Victorian times. The organ gallery was erected in 1991 and replaced a mediaeval musicians' gallery.

In the churchyard there is a grave which records the death of a woman at the age of 133 years.

The Pub
THE CHILDSWICKHAM INN AND BRASSERIE

Is on the Broadway-Childswickham road. This serves bar snacks and also has a full menu.

Organ Loft - St Peters

The Village
ASTON SOMERVILLE . WORCESTERSHIRE
situated a short distance off Broadway-Winchcombe road on
B4632 signposted approx 1½ miles from Broadway

At one time part of Gloucestershire, it was transferred to
Worcestershire when the borders of the counties were altered
in 1931 under a transfer order. The area is mainly farming and
market gardening. There is a social club situated near the church
but there is no pub in the village

The Church
ST MARY THE VIRGIN

Almost hidden from view, being obscured by trees, the approach
is via Church Road, passing the farm buildings. St Mary's is
built of stone in the Norman and transitional styles. It consists
of a chancel, nave, north porch and an embattled tower that has
pinnacles, a clock and bells. The tower, which dates from the 14th
and 15th centuries, has a winding staircase up to the bell chamber.
The pinnacles are believed to have been added during the last
century.

There have been a number of alterations over the centuries
since the church was first built and all that remains of the
original Norman church are the two round piers, which support
the western arch of the nave. These still have the original base.
Alterations were carried out in about 1220 when most of the
church was rebuilt and again during the 14th and 15th centuries.
In the 14th century large windows in the decorated style were put
in the nave, and during the 15th century the east window in the
perpendicular style was inserted.

The roof of the nave has been raised and the screen erected.
The chancel dates from the 13th century with alterations being
carried out in the 15th century. These were to the chancel arch,
the east window and the roof, which was again renewed in 1980.
The floor is not at its original level, but was some six inches
higher. There is a piscina on the south wall and a priest's door.

The altar is modern. The choir stalls are made of oak and date
from the Restoration. The panelling in the sanctuary was made

from the Jacobean box pews, which were once in the nave. There is a mediaeval carved oak chancel screen. The nave has 13th century origins but was raised and had its windows increased in size.

The one time chapel on the south side is no more and a blocked arch is all that remains. The round piers that support the western arch of the nave are probably 12th century. During 1908 the porch was demolished and rebuilt.

On the floor of the church there is a recumbent effigy. This is thought to represent Sir John de Somerville, depicted as a crusader in a suit of chain mail. The effigy has been badly mutilated by locals sharpening knives and shears. This was written of in about 1770, so this vandalism was not done in recent times.

The accurate age of the font is not known but was probably after the Reformation. In 1908 the church was restored and re-seated at a cost of £1,350.

There are various memorials that relate to the Somerville family. It is worth noting that at the west end there is an ancient slab re-used and inscribed to Benjamin Parry of London, goldsmith, d1785.

The Pub

As stated earlier there is no pub in Aston Somerville, the nearest being the **Childswickham Inn and Brasserie**, situated at nearby Childswickham. This establishment serves bar meals and also full menus.

◆ ◆ ◆

Chapter 3

Wickhamford - Worcestershire

◆ ◆ ◆

Bretforton - Worcestershire

The Village
WICKHAMFORD . WORCESTERSHIRE
situated 2½ miles east of Evesham on A44 Evesham-Broadway road

Set in a surroundings of market gardening and farming land, this small village has many dwellings of the 17th/18th centuries. Pretty houses line the road towards the nearby village of Badsey, many of them thatched.

Travelling towards the church which lies on a side road, stands Wickhamford Manor. This superb manor house replaced a previous one that belonged to the abbots of Evesham, whose priory was destroyed by fire. The present building was at one time the home of Sir Samuel Sandy's who bought the manor in 1594.

The manor, when in the abbots' possession, was occupied by Abbot Randolph. When the dissolution of the abbeys took place, the monastic ownership ceased and the Crown took ownership in 1539. The property was then sold off into private hands. The deeds of the property bearing the signature of Queen Elizabeth I. Some 55 years later after passing to various owners, it was then that the Sandy's family took up residence. They lived in the manor until the late 17th century.

The Sandy's family had a close connection with the Washington family, hence the connection between Wickhamford and the United States. Visitors will see evidence of this when visiting the church next to the manor. The beautiful manor is now used as a venue for wedding receptions, corporate events and weekend breaks.

The Church
ST JOHN THE BAPTIST

Was built in the early English style of stone, and consists of an embattled western tower which houses one bell, a chancel, a nave and the south porch. During 1841 the whole church was re-seated and was again restored some 59 years later.

The pulpit is mediaeval and is of three tiers. It was re-panelled in the 17th/18th century. The chancel arch dates from the 13th century and has oak panelling, installed in 1922. The altar table is made in the Jacobean style, but is not Jacobean, although it was carved in oak of that period.

On the north side of the chancel stands a carved oak front, which was a gift from the Sandy's family. Also on the north side is the superb Sandy's monument. This canopied structure is regarded as one of the finest in the area. The double tomb is in alabaster and is placed end to end. The continuous cover is supported by five Corinthian columns. Each tomb has the recumbent figures of a knight and his lady, commemorating Sir Samuel Sandy's with his wife Mercy (Culpeper), and Sir Edwyn Sandy's (Sir Samuel's son) with his wife Penelope (Bulkeley). On the front of the first tomb there are figures of four sons and seven daughters. On the other, there are the figures of five sons and three daughters. The monument was restored in 1956.

The floor monument of Penelope Washington can be seen in front of the altar table. Her great grandfather, Lawrence Washington, was George Washington's great great grandfather. On the monument there is a long Latin inscription, and the Washington family coat of arms, which comprises three stars and two bars. This became the design for the stars and stripes of the United States of America flag. Penelope Washington was the daughter of Colonel Henry Washington, Defender of the City of Worcester for King Charles I.

Above the chancel arch the Stewart Royal Arms can be seen. However, traces of an older coat of arms dating back possibly to the times of James I, are visible. The gallery, taken down in Victorian times, was restored in 1949 by the late George Lees-Milne, who resided at the Manor.

The Pub
SANDY'S ARMS

Built in the early 17th century, this was a coaching inn and once had a blacksmith's adjoining the premises. This one time ale house has seen many changes over the years and is almost rebuilt. It offers bar snacks and has a full menu available.

St John the Baptist - Wickhamford

PEDIGREE OF
THE WASHINGTON FAMILY

JOHN WASHINGTON of Whitfield, Lancashire

JOHN WASHINGTON

ROBERT WASHINGTON
Lancashire • Thrice married • 9 offspring

JOHN WASHINGTON married MARGARET KITSON

LAWRENCE WASHINGTON
Mayor of Northampton 1532-45
Died at Sulgrave 1583

4 Brothers and 1 Sister
(A) 1st. Marriage. No children
(B) 2nd. marriage to ANN PARGITER

ROBERT WASHINGTON

1st. Marriage • 5 brothers
Elizabeth LIGHT • 3 sisters

2nd. Marriage
Ann FISHER, 6 children.

LAWRENCE WASHINGTON married Margaret BUTLER

Sir William WASHINGTON
Married Ann Villiers, half
sister of George, 1st Duke
of Buckingham

JOHN WASHINGTON
Emigrated to America
1657

Lawrence WASHINGTON
Emigrated to America 1657

Margaret W.
Married Sir Robert
Sandys

Alice W
Married Robert
Sandys

Col. Henry WASHINGTON
Fought at the Battle
of Worcester 1651.
Md. Elizabeth Packington

LAWRENCE WASHINGTON
Bridges Creek, Virginia.

Penelope WASHINGTON
Died at WICKHAMFORD
February 27th. 1697

JOHN WASHINGTON   Augustine WASHINGTON
└─ 1st Marriage – 2 sons
┌─ 2nd. Marriage to MARY BALL

GEORGE WASHINGTON
First PRESIDENT U·S·A

3 Brothers
and sisters.

THUS LAWRENCE WASHINGTON the son of Robert Washington and
Elizabeth Light, was the Great Grandfather of Penelope Washington (buried at
Wickhamford) and the Great-Great Grandfather of GEORGE WASHINGTON,
First President of the United States of America.

When Colonel Henry Washington died
his widow, Penelopes mother, married
his friend Samuel Sandys. This is how
Penelope and her mother came to live
at WICKHAMFORD MANOR

The Arms of the
Washington family
became the design
for the 'Stars and
Stripes' of the USA

George Washington family tree

The Village
BRETFORTON . WORCESTERSHIRE
situated approx 4 miles east of Evesham on B4035

A village that was almost entirely built in the 17th century, its Cotswold stone has an ageless appeal, and whilst parking for cars in the village is restricted, there almost always seems to be a space in the village centre. There is a village shop, and a shop called The Ark that sells bric-à-brac.

Up until 1983 there was a Squire of Bretforton. Members of the Ashwin family were squires for some 500 years. The Manor House which was their home stands opposite the church, at the south side.

The Church
ST LEONARD'S

A building in Bretforton was mentioned in the 1066 Domesday Book. There had been one erected in the 8th century, but the present church dates back to c1140-1272 and was built in the transitional to early English, the Gothic, style. It is cruciform. The embattled tower is of the 15th century with pinnacles and gargoyles. It originally housed three bells, but over the centuries this increased to the present six.

Consisting of a chancel, nave, aisles, transeptal chapels, with north and south porches, the church has undergone a number of restorations. In 1847 the chancel and nave were repaired and re-roofed. In 1891 further work was done when the chancel was again the subject of restoration. Upon entry through the south door, which is the oldest part of the building, it will be seen that the restoration has been carried out in different styles, from Norman to late perpendicular.

In 1817 the screen was destroyed, as were several altars and pre-Reformation benches. In 1811 they were replaced and then taken out in 1909. The carved oak choir stalls were brought from Stratford-on-Avon in 1898 and the pine benches in the nave came from Bengeworth Church at Evesham in 1909.

The chancel is late 13th century and was consecrated in 1295. The east window is a copy of the original and was inserted in 1855 in memory of Lt James Collins Ashwin who died in that year. The altar is made of oak and is dated c1611. Only the steps to the rood screen remain. On the south side of the chapel is the priest's door. This was widened in the 15th century.

The transept chapels were added in the 14th century, and in the 15th century the north wall of the north aisle was rebuilt and holy water stoups were inserted. The mutilated remains of a piscina are evident in the south wall of what was the south chapel. These can be seen at the rear of what was the Squire's Pew. The pew itself appears to be Jacobean c1615.

Throughout this lovely church, carvings can be found on the pillars. Visitors are recommended to obtain the Visitor's Guide, available at the church. This gives a detailed description of the carvings and their meanings. The font is believed to date from the 12th century and its lid from the later date of 1721.

The Pub
THE FLEECE INN

Built in mediaeval times as a farmhouse, it was first licensed in 1844 and has been known by various names, The Ark, The Blue Pump and now its present name of The Fleece Inn.

In 1977 it became the property of the National Trust. It was in the will of Lola Taplin, who was the owner and licensee. It was her intention that it remain as an unspoilt village inn. With its flagstone floors and low beams, it is evident that her wish is being carried out.

The Fleece has an appeal to visitors from all parts of the world. It has been used in the making of a number of films, including the TV version of Martin Chuzzlewit. Bar snacks are available and a full menu.

◆ ◆ ◆

Chapter 4

Bishops Cleeve - Gloucestershire

◆ ◆ ◆

Woolstone - Gloucestershire

The Village
BISHOP'S CLEEVE . GLOUCESTERSHIRE
3 miles north of Cheltenham on A435 Evesham road

The village has grown considerably over recent years, but the centre has retained the atmosphere of a smaller village. It is well served with shops and other amenities. Unusually for a village these days, there is a ladies dress shop. Smith's industries is a major employer in the area.

The Church
ST MICHAEL AND ALL ANGELS

It is believed that the original building was of Saxon origin and was destroyed by the Danes. No trace of the church from those times remains. It was rebuilt by the Normans in about 1170. Parts of the original Norman church that remain are the nave, the transepts, the porch and upper porch room, the latter being considered rare. The porch as stated is Norman, and as was the custom of the times, would have been used for part of the wedding and baptism services.

Upon entering the nave, visitors will observe a very substantial Jacobean musicians' gallery, almost certainly gifted to the church by the de la Bere family in 1604, replacing an earlier one.

It can also be observed that in the nave, every other pillar has been removed. This was done in the 16th/17th century. The north aisle was extended in c1300 and new windows put in place. It is worth mentioning that Christ is depicted as having six toes. This was due to a repair being done and the error apparently not being noticed at the time. The north transept is Norman, with the north window installed c1305. Originally a chantry chapel, the recess then housed the altar. The stairway to the belfry is one of the oldest in use and is of 15th century origin.

The chancel was extended to its present form c1280 and has a priest's door in the south wall. The east window is dated 1900. The tower was rebuilt in 1700 after falling down in 1696. The rood screen and loft were removed following the Reformation. A rood cross now hangs above the chancel. This was painted and donated in 1987 by PJ Crook, an artist and member of the parish.

The south transept is Norman and the window was put in c1305. An effigy of an unknown knight c1270 is in the recess beneath the window. The piscina is Norman and has a cruet shelf above it. The south aisle chantry was added in c1310. Beside the de la Bere monument there is a double piscina and the recess is believed to have housed the founder's tomb or effigy. The windows were replaced c1450.

The evidence is that the upper porch room was built in the early 13th century and was at that time detached from the main body of the church. It was probably used as living quarters by a priest. Some time during the 15th/16th century it was joined to the church. The room has a history of being used as a schoolroom. There are records confirming that a priest or clerk was acting as a schoolmaster and licensed to teach as far back as 1572. Wall painting decorates the walls and would have been done by the schoolmaster of the period. The rules of the academy are painted on the wall to the left of the window, and to the right there is a skeleton portrayed. On the east and west walls there is a battle scene and paintings of a lion and tiger. The upper porch room is well worth a visit and is very much a picture of the education system in the 1800s.

St Michael and All Angels once had the largest parsonage in the country. This building now contains offices.

Wall painting - St Michael & All Angels

The Pub

there are four

THE KING'S HEAD
Cheltenham Road

This is a 17th century building, previously cottages. It became a pub in late Victorian times. The building is Grade II listed. Bar snacks are served and a full menu is available.

The Kings Head - Bishops Cleeve

THE ROYAL OAK
Church Road

This is also a 17th century building. It has had a number of alterations, including one that extended into the next door barber's shop. It is a Grade II listed building. Bar snacks are served and a full menu is available.

THE SWALLOW INN
Bishop's Drive

This is a modern pub, named after a sailing dingy. Serves bar snacks.

THE CROWN AND HARP
Cheltenham Road

Licensed in the early 19th century. Serves bar snacks.

◆ ◆ ◆

The Village
WOOLSTONE . GLOUCESTERSHIRE
situated off Evesham-Cheltenham road A435
2 miles north of Bishop's Cleeve

This tiny village, consisting of just a few houses and farms, nestles into the hillside and is on a no-through road.

The Church
ST MARTIN DE TOURS

It is believed that the original structure was possibly Saxon, but there are no records of when the church was first built and consecrated. It was, however, restored and partly rebuilt in 1499 and there was further reconstruction in Victorian times.

The church consists of a tower, nave and chancel. There is evidence of a north aisle in earlier times, for on the north wall there are three pointed arches, supported by pillars, that are now filled with stonework.

The perpendicular tower has corner buttresses and a battlemented top with gargoyles that date back to the 15th century. There is a peal of six bells. Originally there were three until 1974. The oldest bell is dated 1678 and was the work of Toby Morris of Stamford. The tower has a distinct lean to west and south, and has been required to be underpinned.

In the nave near the south door stands the font, which is perpendicular in style and has an octagonal bowl. On the north wall there are two modern windows of two lights in the decorated style. A small door o the north side of the chancel leads to the vestry. This was erected in 1975. A modern two light window matching the one in the nave is also on the north side. The east window is the oldest and has been very well preserved. It is of curvilinear tracery and has three lights. The decorated glass was put in during 1907 and is to the memory of the Rev DGG Coventry, who was the priest for 37 years.

There are canopied niches on the east wall each side of the window, the northern one being badly mutilated. The southern one is, however, in better condition. It has a perpendicular canopy. On the floor of the niche there is a carved stone pillar about one meter in height, believed to have been part of the pillars which once supported the arches in the north aisle.

The effigy is that of a priest. There is no tomb, but it is known that Woolstone was attached to the Priory at Deerhurst in 1271. As the effigy possibly dates back to the late 14th century, it is more than likely that there is a connection between the effigy and Deerhurst. The priest's chair is made of rough black oak and is dated about 1640. A window similar to that in the nave is in the south wall. The pews and pulpit are modern.

Following the Battle of Tewkesbury in 1471, the church was re-consecrated. This was due to two soldiers of the defeated Lancastrian army being pursued by Yorkist soldiers. The fleeing soldiers sought refuge at the church, but the Yorkists ignored the conventions of sanctuary and put the Lancastrians to death. The re-consecration crosses are etched on the wall on the outside of the tower and on the inside wall of the sanctuary.

The Pub

There is no pub in Woolstone, but a short distance away on the A435 just outside Bishop's Cleeve is the Old Farmers Arms. Built in 1853 as an alehouse, the pub was used by coaches travelling from Cheltenham to Evesham. Horses were rested and watered and passengers were able to take refreshments in the bar. As well as coaches and carriages, there were many carriers' wagons taking goods to the various markets in the area who would call in. It was also a place where 'Mummers', a travelling group of players, would stop to entertain. They would accept the landlord's hospitality, would duly perform, and then pass a hat round.

In 1833 the local Friendly Society met at the Old Farmers Arms. Each week members would pay their subscriptions, consisting of just a few pennies, so that they could obtain cash benefits in the event of them being ill. There was also a funeral benefit.

In present times the pub is popular with travellers and locals. It serves snacks and also has an extensive menu.

◆ ◆ ◆

Chapter 5

Bredon - Worcestershire

◆ ◆ ◆

Beckford - Worcestershire

◆ ◆ ◆

Ashton-Under-Hill
         - Worcestershire

The Village
BREDON . WORCESTERSHIRE
situated 3 miles north of Tewkesbury on B4080

At the south east of Bredon Hill, this village has many links with the past. Upon the hill itself there is evidence of an encampment dating back to Roman times. Houses within Bredon are of 16th/17th century construction and varying dates up to present times. There are Cotswold stone dwellings, thatched and modern.

Amenities in the village include two shops, a pottery and a teddy bear shop. A pleasant picnic site can be found on the banks of the river. This can be reached by taking the road past the church.

The Church
ST GILES

Has origins dating back to the latter part of the 12th century. It is constructed of stone and has an embattled central tower with a spire that rises to 160ft. The tower houses five bells.

In the body of the church there is the chancel, nave, south chapel, north chapel, north aisle and porch. The church contains five building styles. It can be seen that these are as follows: Norman, Early English, Decorated, Perpendicular and Modern. The nave, porch, south west and north doorways are Norman. The south aisle is early English with perpendicular, and the north aisle and chancel is of the decorated style.

Upon entering through the north door, the structure of the porch can be seen. It consists of diagonal ribs. All entrances are decorated with a chevron ornament, as was the custom of the times. The commencement of weddings and christenings would have been held in the porch.

In the nave, Norman windows face each other from the north and south walls, and the remains of a piscina can be found. In the north and south walls of the chancel, windows have decorated tracery. A piscina and triple sedilia will be observed. Also to be found east of the tomb without an inscription is an aumbry.

Against the south wall of the sanctuary, in an upright position, there is a 14th century coffin lid. This was discovered many years

Crucifix - St Giles, Bredon

ago in the floor face down. The carving is believed to represent members of the Reed, or Reede, family. In the north wall there is an Easter Sepulchre.

The tower is separated from the nave by a rood screen. There are several monuments to be found, one of which commemorates William and Katherine Reed and their child. This is situated to the west side of the sanctuary south of the chancel.

In the west of the south aisle, the magnificent memorial to Sir Giles and Lady Katherine Reed stands, both of whom died in 1611. It is of black marble and has recumbent effigies of both, with kneeling figures of their children. This superb memorial is lavishly decorated.

The Pub

there are two

THE FOX AND HOUNDS

This picturesque inn, which is thatched and timbered, has 16th century origins and although refurbished and extended, has retained its old-world charms. A full à la carte menu is available.

The Fox & Hounds - Bredon

THE ROYAL OAK

This is an old coaching inn and is believed to have been built at some time in the 14th/15th century. It has been refurbished in recent times but has retained some of its original character. Bar meals are available and overnight guests are catered for.

◆ ◆ ◆

The Village
BECKFORD . WORCESTERSHIRE
signposted off A46 road approx 6 miles south of Evesham

Consisting of many 17th century houses, although not a large village, it is a village of much activity. The Vale Wild Life Centre has a rescue facility which is open to visitors. The village has a post office and stores, and is also the home of Beckford Silk. This company's workshops, where screen printing is carried out, are open to the public. Visitors can observe the various processes being carried out. There is a shop where items of silk can be purchased. This has much appeal to visitors, many of them from overseas. Within the building there is a coffee shop serving home made meals and cakes, always worth a visit.

Beckford has also had its share of history. The Rev John Trimbrill, Archdeacon of Gloucester, was vicar from 1797 to 1865 and it was during this period, it is said, that he was called upon to make a decision regarding a young man caught sheep stealing. He had the option of dealing with the case in his capacity as a magistrate or sending the offender to the assizes, with the knowledge that if found guilty at the assizes, the sentence would be death. The Rev Trimbrill referred him to the assizes and the young man was subsequently executed. Had the case been dealt with by magistrates there would have been a lesser sentence awarded. It was believed that as a result of this action the people of the nearby village of Aston Under Hill set up the Free Church in protest.

Was this fact or fiction? It is recorded, however, that the Rev Trimbrill did attend the Northleach House of Correction in his capacity as a magistrate for Gloucestershire and Worcestershire. The fine 17th century vicarage is now privately owned but evidence of the Trimbrill family remains. Two of the bedroom windows have children's names etched into the glass.

The village holds an annual fête with many attractions. This usually takes place in the first week of July. There is a tennis club.

The Church
ST JOHN THE BAPTIST

St John the Baptist has Saxon origins. This was revealed during restoration work being carried out in 1911 when Saxon foundations were uncovered. The embattled tower houses six bells. Upon entering the porch, which was probably erected during the 15th century, stone benches can be observed. Before the days of pews, benches such as these would have lined three sides of the nave.

Before entering the church, which is through the south doorway, visitors should take a close look at the superb example of the architecture of the time. The tympanum depicts an animal adoring the Holy Trinity. The eye represents the Father, the cross the Son, the dove the Holy Ghost. The animals were regarded as sacred beasts.

The church consists of a nave and chancel. Two of the original Norman windows are opposite each other. Near the west end the remains of the windows can be seen. In the north wall near the pulpit, there is an early English window consisting of two lights. By the door on the south wall there is a two light early decorated window and one of perpendicular style. The octagonal font is of the 15th century.

The north door has been blocked up and the recess formed has been used to position a war memorial to members of the parish who fell in the two World Wars. The tower arch of the nave displays another example of 12th century Norman architecture. On the outer column of the north side, there are two demon-like heads and a centaur. A large part of the column on the south side was removed when a triple decked pulpit was put in, probably in the 18th century.

The tower was built in three stages and was erected in three different periods. It was at the end of the 13th century when it was decided to enlarge the chancel. This was done by using the walls at the base of the tower and a new chancel was built. The old chancel walls were buttressed and the middle section of the tower was built between 1310 and 1315. A further section was built in 1622 when it replaced a decayed wooden spire.

The chancel has a Queen post roof. Four lancet windows remain. The one on the south side was replaced by one of the

Screen printing - Beckford Silk, Beckford

The coffee shop - Beckford Silk, Beckford

decorated style. A window on the north side was blocked up when the chantry was built. The chancel screen is modern but incorporates the remnants of an older screen.

The Pub
THE BECKFORD INN & HOTEL

Built in the 18th century as a coaching inn, the Beckford has been extended and refurbished many times over the years, but maintains many of its original features. Nowadays it caters for overnight guests, has conference facilities and hosts other functions. Bar snacks are available and a full menu. Adjoining the hotel there is a field with provision for caravans.

◆ ◆ ◆

ASHTON UNDER HILL . WORCESTERSHIRE
signposted off the Evesham - Cheltenham road A46
and is a short distance from Beckford

The building style in this village covers a range of 17th century houses, some built of Cotswold stone, others in black and white timber frame. The village has developed over the years and this is reflected in a mixture of old and new properties. However, the oldest dwelling is believed to be a farmhouse which dates back to the 15th century.

At one time the area was noted for its fruit growing, but this has now gone. Piped water did not arrive in the village until after World War II. Water was obtained from private wells prior to this. There are many activities within the village, which include a cricket team and a thriving amateur dramatic society. The late Fred Archer, author, lived here for most of his life. In his books he wrote about life in and around Ashton many years ago. A local resident, Joe Aspey, has written a book about walks which is entitled 'Walks from Ashton Under Hill'.

Each year an open garden day is held, and a village fête once every two years. There are two schools, the village school and a middle school.

At one time the village belonged in Gloucestershire. It was transferred to Worcestershire in 1931.

The Church

there are two

ST BARBARA

Approaching the church there is an ancient cross at the roadside. This consists of three steps, a shaft and a sundial, which replaces the original top.

St Barbara is one of only four churches of that name in the country. Built of stone in the early style with traces of later work, it has a western tower which is embattled with pinnacles and gargoyles. As with many towers, it was built in two stages, the lower part in the 13th century and the upper part being added in the 15th century.

Entry into the church is gained via the south porch. This is 14th century and contains the remains of a stoup in the east wall, which at one time would have held Holy water. In 1903 the porch was taken down and rebuilt, as it was falling into disrepair. The south doorway is Norman with rounded arch and single shafts, the capitals being scalloped.

Upon entry into the church, the Victorian restoration is obvious. The pine pews, oak pulpit and reading desk were installed at that time. The original north wall of the nave has been removed and replaced with four perpendicular style arches, which give access to the north aisle. An enlargement of the church took place when, in 1868, the schoolroom which was attached to the north aisle was removed. The font stands in the north aisle and is of the 15th century, its cover of the 19th century.

The chancel was largely rebuilt by Sir John Franklin, who was Lord of the Manor in 1624, the chancel arch being rebuilt in the early 19th century in a style to match the four arches.

The east window has stained glass which is dated 1879. This shows a representation of the crucifixion across the three lancets. The three side windows date from 1912 and depict the four Evangelists on the south side, with St Cecilia and St Barbara on the north. The communion table is Jacobean.

The south wall of the nave is Norman with each of the four windows dating from different periods. The single lancet window at the rear of the organ was installed when the 19th century restoration was being carried out, but it has been done in 13th century style. The four-lancet window is dated c1500 and is in the perpendicular style. The double lancet window near the door is 14th century. This contains a roundel of mediaeval glass and has an heraldic shield in the foliated head. The arms are that of the Cheyne family, who held the Priory of Beckford 1379-1437. Sir John Cheyne was Speaker of the House of Commons. The remaining window is in the west end. This is almost certainly the oldest window and originates from the 13th century. It is a simple lancet with cusped top.

There are several memorials to the Baldwyn family and an unusual 17th century monument on the south wall of the chancel.

The Priest Door - St Barbara's, Ashton-Under-Hill

It contains an epitaph to an unknown person. The register of marriages and burials dates from 1586.

Outside the church on the south side there is a priest's door with a plaque above it commemorating the rebuilding. It shows a date of Anno Domini 1624. Above the chancel east window there are some interesting carvings which feature two dolphins.

THE FREE CHURCH

In 1881 the church was built on land given by a Mr New, who was a solicitor of Evesham. Previously services were conducted in private houses within the village. In 1924 the church was given to the congregation. It contains a memorial window of stained glass, which was installed to the memory of those killed in the First World War.

The Pub
THE STAR INN

at one time the village had three pubs

The Plough Inn closed about 1940
The White Hart closed some time before the Second World War

Originally built as three cottages in 1660, The Star Inn was converted into a pub beyond living memory. It retains many of its features from that period. Its Jacobean style is attractive. A full menu is available, but on certain days only, so it is advisable to check.

♦ ♦ ♦

Chapter 6

Inkberrow - Worcestershire

◆ ◆ ◆

Fladbury - Worcestershire

◆ ◆ ◆

Cropthorne - Worcestershire

◆ ◆ ◆

Elmley Castle - Worcestershire

The Village
INKBERROW . WORCESTERSHIRE
situated midway between Worcester and
Stratford-upon-Avon on A422

A large village with a substantial amount of modern housing, although it is easy to see what the old village comprised. There are many 16th/17th century houses, some of which overlook the village green. A post office and general store serves some of the needs of the community. The busy A422 runs through the village and was an old coaching route.

On the left of the road leading to the church, a large building can be seen. This was the old vicarage. It was sold into private ownership in 1946 and was converted into two houses. On 10 May 1645 Charles I spent the night in the old vicarage. He was en route to Droitwich with his army. An old map book of his was found and is now held in the county archives. It is believed that his troops' wages were lost and were buried in or around the village. It is said that as an act of revenge for housing Charles, Cromwell's soldiers set fire to the vicarage.

In the village there is a tennis club and a bowls club.

The Church
ST PETER'S

Built of stone in the perpendicular and decorated style, it consists of a chancel, nave, north aisle, south transept and north porch. There is an embattled western tower with pinnacles. This houses six bells and a clock.

Entry into the church is through the north porch, which was added in the 15th century. Large gargoyles adorn the porch. There have been several restorations and alterations. In 1390 the chancel was rebuilt and the floor re-laid. In the 16th century the north aisle was extended over the vestry. In Victorian times the east and south walls were again rebuilt, the south wall being moved outwards.

It is thought that the south transept could have been added as a chantry chapel shortly after 1357 to pray for the souls of the Colman family of Dormston. However, the only part that remains is the arch, as the chapel was rebuilt and extended.

In the south transept under a canopy of marble is an altar tomb to the memory of John Savage Esq JP. He died on 11 December 1635. Over the canopy is an achievement of arms. His recumbent effigy is believed to have been vandalised by Cromwell's troops. The feet and hands are missing, as are the heads of the kneeling figures of his ten children, which adorn the sides of the base.

The nave is Norman and is part of the original building. It was altered between the late 14th and 15th century. The window nearest the tower contains 15th century stained glass. The font is Norman and stands at the western end, being moved to that position in Victorian times. The original 13th century vestry was located where the present St Catherine's Chapel is. It was moved to its present location in 1968. It was screened off using oak panelling by Pancheri.

Looking at the carvings on the south side of the screen, Charles I is depicted in armour before the Battle of Edgehill. If you take a careful look, you will see that Charles' head is detached from his body. The stained glass in the window of the west wall of the vestry is 15th century and depicts St Catherine and one other saint.

The Old Bull - Inkberrow

Vestry Screen, Beheaded Charles I - St Peters, Inkberrow

The Pub

there are two

THE OLD BULL

Is believed to have been a coach house in 1527. In the deeds to the property it is shown that it has been a public house since at least 1750. The story is told that William Shakespeare took refreshments here whilst on his way to obtain his marriage bond in Worcester.

The Old Bull is well known as being 'The Bull' at Ambridge in the Radio 4 serial 'The Archers'. Timber framed, with wooden beams, flagstone floors and log fires, it has an old-world atmosphere. Bar snacks are available.

THE BULL'S HEAD INN

Was once known as 'The George'. It has origins dating from 1649 and was a coaching inn. It now has five letting bedrooms and a function room which can be hired. Flagstone floors and low beams add to its charm. Bar snacks and a full menu are available.

◆ ◆ ◆

The Village
FLADBURY . WORCESTERSHIRE
approx equidistant between Evesham and Pershore 3-3½ miles to each. Travel on A44 and follow direction sign to village

This attractive village stands close to the River Avon. It displays a number of building styles reflecting different periods of construction. There are many ancient properties.

It was one of the earliest villages in the area to have electricity. This was introduced to the village in 1899. It was in 1898 that LH Elkington, a chartered accountant who resided at the Manor House, arranged with the mill owner George Stephens, to provide a supply of electricity to his home. So it was in 1899 that it was decided to offer power to the whole village. A company was formed and named The Fladbury Electric Light and Power Co Ltd in the following years. The company changed hands and was sold to SWS Electric Supply Co in 1927.

At the outset electricity was supplied to seven street lights for a limited number of hours. In 1902, with an increased population, the mill was generating power to 280 lamps. Over the years the mill has ground flour and been used in cider making. The mill, situated by the river weir, is of the 16th century and probably replaced an earlier more primitive one that was recorded in the Domesday Book. Although it is no longer a working mill, it attracts the artist and photographer for its 'Constable' appeal. The river also attracts fishermen, the boating fraternity and visitors who just enjoy the peaceful setting.

The Jubilee Bridge over the river connects Fladbury with the neighbouring villages of Cropthorne and Charlton. A bridge was built in 1889-1891, the present one being constructed in 1933 but still retaining the name of Jubilee. The surrounding area is used for farming and market gardening.

Evesham Golf Club is situated on the Evesham-Wyre Piddle road, as is Craycombe House. This was the one time home of the late Francis Brett Young, the novelist.

Each year in July, the village has a festival and walkabout. This annual event includes a flower festival in the church, villagers gardens are open, there are stalls, children's activities, entertainers and many other attractions.

The Church
ST JOHN THE BAPTIST

There was a settlement at Fladbury in the 7th century when monks settled in the area. These subsequently moved to Evesham and founded the monastery that became Evesham Abbey. No evidence of the Saxon church has remained.

The present building consists of a chancel, nave, aisles, south porch and a west embattled tower, which contains eight bells. The lower part of the tower is Norman and the upper part is of the 17th century. Before entering the porch, which is 14th century and renovated in the 17th century, observe the mediaeval scratch sundial.

In the 18th century oak pews were installed. The ceiling is Georgian. Mediaeval tiles decorate two positions in the north and south walls. The remains of a canopied piscina can be seen on the south wall.

The chancel was restored in Victorian times, and the chancel arch, the east and south walls, date from that period. A reredos of alabaster and mosaic with figures of angels extends over the whole of the east end. The stained glass east window was presented by John Cartwright Esq of Craycombe House.

In the sanctuary there is a double piscina in the south wall. In the north wall of the chancel the de Montford memorial window of 15th century glass can be seen. It shows the shields of Henry III and six barons and knights slain at the Battle of Evesham 1265. It is thought that the glass originated from Evesham Abbey and was brought to Fladbury following the Dissolution of the Monasteries.

Besides various memorial tablets, the altar tomb of John Throckmorton, Sub Treasurer of Britain OB 1445, his wife Eleanor (de Spineto) and their son Thomas, stands at the west end. The tomb is of polished Purbeck marble and has brass effigies.

The Pub

there are two

THE ANCHOR

Dates from 1647. Its name was taken from the time when there was a wharf on the nearby River Avon and barges were anchored there. It has original beams. The premises have been tastefully refurbished and offer bar snacks and a full menu.

Both pubs have an interesting history. In 1877 The Chequers passed into the ownership of Eleanor Sarah Hundy upon the death of her father. Eleanor and her new husband Albert were so successful in their enterprise, that they eventually acquired The Anchor inn. They had the Misses Fanny and Emily Foster to manage it for them. Over the years ownership has changed many times and the pubs are now separately owned.

Cropthorne Mill - Fladbury

THE CHEQUERS

Is believed to originate from the early 15th century and is the older of the two, with low beams and an original fireplace with brass kettles and fire irons. Log fires in the colder weather. There are bar snacks available and a full menu. Overnight guests are welcome.

◆ ◆ ◆

The Chequers - Fladbury

Cropthorne Mill - Fladbury

The Village
CROPTHORNE . WORCESTERSHIRE
situated equidistant between Evesham and Pershore 3 miles from
each. Travel on B4084 to reach village

Situated on the opposite side of the river to Fladbury, which can be
reached via the Jubilee Bridge, Cropthorne once had a mill. This
and Fladbury mill were both at one time owned by the Church.
Cropthorne mill was known as The Parsonage Mill and, as the
name indicates, it belonged to the parsonage. It was recorded
in Domesday Book, but the present building is 16th century. It
ceased working and passed into private hands.

The village has many fine houses, timber framed and thatched.
The black and white properties are most attractive. An important
building is Holland House. This was originally three cottages and
was altered into a farmhouse in the early 19th century. In 1820 it
was purchased by an eminent surgeon Sir William Lawson Tait.
Upon his death it was bought by Mr HH Avery of Birmingham.
In 1920 the property went into the ownership of Mrs Ellis
Holland. At the end of the Second World War Mrs Holland gave
the house to the Diocese of Worcester and since then it has been
used as a retreat and conference house.

The Church
ST MICHAEL

Was built about 1100 and is almost certainly on the site of an
earlier Saxon church. It consists of a chancel, nave, aisles, south
porch and an embattled tower with pinnacles and gargoyles. The
tower is of three stages, the two lower parts are of the 12th century
and the upper part is 15th century. Built of stone, the church is in
the Gothic style. The south porch was rebuilt in the 16th century
from old materials.

Upon entry into the church, the most prominent features
immediately confront the visitor. These are the monuments to the
Dingley, or Dineley, family. These are superb monuments. One is
to Edward Dingley and his lady 1646. There are kneeling effigies
of both, as well as their four sons and three daughters. The other
monument is to Francis Dingley and Elizabeth his wife 1624. It

has recumbent effigies with an inscription and pedigree of the family. It has the kneeling figures of nineteen sons and daughters, proceeding through the chancel arch, which was built in the early 12th century, just a few years before the tower was added.

To the rear of the altar is a marble reredos. This was erected by the children of Francis Dermot Holland, who was a lay rector and was responsible for the restoration of the chancel in 1894. In the north wall of the sanctuary there is a small lancet window of c1200. The painted figure of St Michael is modern. On the south side of the sanctuary there is a pedestal piscina of the 13th century.

It was during the rebuilding of the chancel that an ancient runic cross c800 with elaborate carvings was discovered, built into the south wall of the sanctuary. Also discovered was an altar slab bearing five consecration crosses. The runic cross is on display in the Lady Chapel. The east window in the Lady Chapel is of fine clear glass. Beneath it is the ancient stone slab. The reredos is modern and was erected in 1932 to the memory of Colonel Ellis Holland. To the left of the altar there is a piscina.

The pillars and arches in the nave are the oldest part and are of

Edward Dimley & Wife, 1646 - St Michael's Cropthorne

the 12th century. Following this was the arcade on the south side. In the latter part of the 1400s alterations were carried out in this part of the church. The celestory windows in the north side are 18th century in design and those in the south side are of the 15th century. The font is Victorian.

The Pub

there are two

THE BELL

Once three cottages, then a farm, it became a coaching inn. It has been refurbished and serves bar snacks with a full menu. It can provide for overnight guests. It is believed to be about 200 years old. Interesting features in The Bell are the many wall paintings.

THE NEW INN

Is of about the same age. It has a skittle alley. Bar snacks are served and a full menu is available.

Holland House - Cropthorne

The Village
ELMLEY CASTLE . WORCESTERSHIRE
situated off Evesham-Pershore road on B4084
travelling from Evesham turn left shortly after passing
The Bell Inn at Cropthorne
travelling from Pershore turn right after passing over bridge
follow direction signs to Elmley Castle

The village stands at the foot of the Bredon Hills. It is bounded on the east and south east by the county of Gloucestershire. It contains many picturesque houses of the 16th century. Some of the village water supply still comes from the Bredon Hills.

The castle itself was the seat of General Sir Francis John Davies and was built shortly after the Norman Conquest. It was destroyed in the War of the Barons during the reign of Henry III and only some of the foundations of the original castle still exist, the stone being removed to build in the village and also used in the construction of the bridge at Pershore.

There are the remains of the old market cross in the village. A shop and post office operate two days a week at the new Village Hall.

The Church
ST MARY'S

This is built of stone and consists of a chancel, nave, aisles, north porch and an embattled western tower which houses six bells and a clock. The church has its origins in the late 11th century, at that time consisting only of a chancel and nave. In the 13th, 14th and 15th centuries major alterations were carried out in the following sequence: the lower part of the tower was erected, the north transept and south aisle was added, the upper part of the tower was built.

Entering the embattled north porch, carvings of animals can be seen on each side. These are believed to be of the 11th and 12th centuries. Also in the wall are the remains of a stoup.

Upon entry into the church, pews of the 16th century will be observed. During the restoration carried out in 1878 when the nave and aisles were newly roofed, some Norman carvings and painted wall decorations were discovered. At the same time a coped tombstone with a 13th century cross was found beneath the floor. It was during this restoration that all internal plaster was removed from the walls.

Going to the north transept, the superb memorial to the Savage family occupies the larger part. The memorial is carved in alabaster and shows the recumbent effigies of Sir William Savage died 1616, Sir Giles Savage died 1631, and Lady Catherine Savage died 1674. She holds an infant daughter. The four sons kneel at the foot of the memorial. Also in the north transept is the Coventry Memorial which is to Thomas, first Earl of Coventry.

In the sanctuary a 14th century doorway has been partly walled up. The remains of a 14th century piscina are to be found in the east wall. The font is octagonal and stands at the west end of the centre aisle. The pedestal is of particular interest. It has coiled figures of dragons and is believed to be of the 11th/12th century. There are a number of memorial tablets in various parts of the church.

The Pub

there are two

THE QUEEN ELIZABETH

Built in about 1460-1480, it was originally three cottages. The signboard is unique. It was painted from portraits of Queen Elizabeth I, who visited Elmley Castle on 20 August 1575 and was received by the then Lord of the Manor, General Sir Francis John Davies.

The cricket team meets at this venue.

THE OLD MILL INN

Built in the 18th century, The Old Mill Inn has long been conducting its business as an inn. When it was a working mill, water from Bredon Hill fed the three pools which powered the mill wheel.

What was the mill owner's house and granary is now the

present Old Mill Inn, which caters for overnight guests. At one time the bar consisted of only one room. Beer was brought up from barrels kept in the cellar and was served from jugs. It was then just an alehouse.

Two ghosts are reputed to haunt in and around The Old Mill, one being a child that was believed to have drowned in the mill pool, the other being the upper part of a lady. The current licensee says that other licensees before him have experienced seeing the apparitions.

The pathway between the inn and the mill pool is known as Death Walk. This name originates from the time when coffins were taken along this route to the church.

The pub serves bar snacks and has a full menu available.

◆ ◆ ◆

Carving - St Mary's, Elmley Castle

Part 2

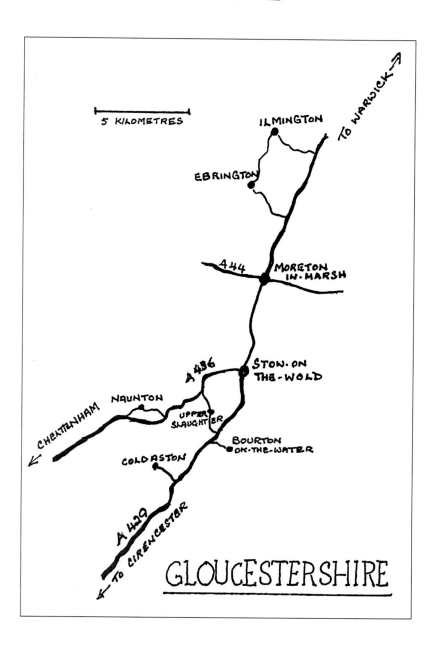

5 KILOMETRES

ILMINGTON

TO WARWICK →

EBRINGTON

A44

MORETON
IN·MARSH

A436

STOW·ON
THE·WOLD

NAUNTON

CHELTENHAM

UPPER
SLAUGHTER

BOURTON
ON·THE·WATER

COLD ASTON

A 429

TO CIRENCESTER

GLOUCESTERSHIRE

Chapter 7

Cold Aston - Gloucestershire

◆ ◆ ◆

Upper Slaughter
- Gloucestershire

◆ ◆ ◆

Naunton - Gloucestershire

The Village
COLD ASTON . GLOUCESTERSHIRE
(once known as Aston Blank)
situated a short distance away from Northleach
Cold Aston can be reached via A429 Northleach-Morton in
Marsh road signposted approx 2½ miles north of Northleach

A pleasant village which has a large oak tree dominating the area near The Plough public house. The village is well spread, with the church at one end and the pub at the other. It has typical village activities, with an annual fête taking place, usually on the first Saturday in August.

There are stalls that line the street, selling all sorts of home made produce, pickles, jams, cakes, etc. The church normally has a theme and is decorated accordingly. Dancers put on displays and a brass (or silver) band plays, usually positioned under the large tree. It has also been known to have a dog show, a very light hearted affair. Teas and soft drinks are on sale, as are ice creams and other refreshments. The day finishes with an evening function. A truly traditional village fête.

The Church
ST ANDREW

It was in 1287 that the Bishop of Worcester inducted a priest to 'Aston Frigida', and following this, documents show that the village was known as Aston Frigida or Cold Aston. In 1554 the patent roll declared the appointment of a vicar to Aston Blank. This name is not in evidence prior to that date. Before 1554 vicars of Cold Aston had been appointed by the priors of Malvern. It was upon the Dissolution of the Monasteries that the right presentation passed to the crown.

The church itself has largely been restored. The entrance is through the south doorway, which is Norman. The tympanum has an arch with rosettes. The nave wall is mainly Norman and the corbels are of mediaeval men and women. The roof beams are of the 19th century.

The niche in the north wall is a blocked up Norman doorway. The chancel arch was part of the Restoration in 1875. There are the remains of an early English piscina and the reredos is of 14th century origin. The Easter Sepulchre on the north wall was made from a 14th century niche. At the west end of the nave is the 15th century bell tower. The tower is perpendicular with diagonal buttress and has a Tudor doorway on the west side.

The yew tree standing by the gate is more than 600 years old and has a 16ft girth.

The Pub
THE PLOUGH INN

Built in the 17th century, and despite alterations, has managed to hold on to its old-world charm. With its flagstone floor and low ceilings, it has all the atmosphere of the typical village pub. At one time it also served as the village shop and post office.

Until the 1950s there were two pubs in the village, the other being The Keeper's Arms. This closed when it was purchased by the brewery, who already owned The Plough Inn.

Bar snacks are served and a full menu is available.

◆ ◆ ◆

The Village
UPPER SLAUGHTER . GLOUCESTERSHIRE
situated off B4048 between Stow on the Wold and Andoversford
Upper Slaughter is signposted a short distance along this road
from Stow

This peaceful village built of Cotswold stone has few buildings that are new. The River Windrush flows through the village and there is a ford which seems to attract many visitors, its clear water flowing endlessly.

In Norman times Upper Slaughter boasted a castle, although there is little evidence of this nowadays. To the east of the church lies what is known as the Castle Mound. The Castle appears to have been built mainly of wood, with stone walls around the Keep.

The original manor house became the present Lord of the Manor Hotel. It was constructed in the late 16th century over a 15th century building.

At the centre of this gem of a village is The Square. This was reconstructed in 1906 by Sir Edward Lutyens, the well known architect.

The Church
ST PETER'S

This may have been used as part of the defences of the village in the 12th century, as there were stories, unauthenticated, of a tunnel between the castle and the church. Evidence exists of the church having 12th century origins, as a window in the tower has been dated back to that time.

During the year of the Civil War, a considerable amount of damage was done to the church. In the 14th century the chancel was rebuilt, very much as can be seen today. Following this in the 15th century, the upper part of the tower was rebuilt. In the 18th century the clock was installed. A number of alterations were made in the succeeding century when the north aisle was added. The mortuary chapel was built and houses the tomb of the Reverend Witts, of 'Diary of a Cotswold Parson' fame, who died in 1854.

Upon entering the church through the south door, remnants of the Norman tympanum can be seen. A copy of the original font stands to the west in front of the bell ringing chamber. In close vicinity stands the original font. One had been removed for some unknown reason. It was later found and returned to the church.

The roll of rectors of the parish is shown on the north wall. The Witts Memorial Chapel is at the east end of the north aisle. In this area the unused spiral staircase to the organ loft is situated. On the north wall of the chancel, it can be seen that the Easter Sepulchre has been filled in with the Baroque tomb of Frances and Andrew Wanley of Eyford, bearing the date of 1682. In the south wall of the chancel there is a piscina and the Slaughter family arms are displayed.

The bell tower houses five bells, three of which are 19th century, one 18th century and the fifth bell is known as the 'Eleanor' bell. It has been stamped with the heads of King Edward I and Queen Eleanor, who died in 1290.

The Pub

There is no pub in Upper Slaughter. However, just a short distance away in Lower Swell, the **Gold Ball Inn** can be found. This pub has its origins in the 17th century, when it was a private house. It became licensed premises over 110 years ago and has retained many of its original features, such as exposed stone walls and black beams. A bar menu is available. The inn also offers accommodation.

◆ ◆ ◆

The Village
NAUNTON . GLOUCESTERSHIRE
situated approx 5 miles from Stow on the Wold
take B4068 from which Naunton is signposted

Described as a village where time has stood still, Naunton has centuries of history. With its cottages built in Cotswold stone it has a beauty so typical of the area. There are traces of the Bronze Age and of the Roman occupation 300AD. Foundations of Roman Villas and graves of Roman soldiers, along with coins and pottery, have been found.

As with most of the Cotswolds, sheep farming played a major part in the wealth of the village. In the 16th century the village provided employment for a blacksmith, two tailors and a butcher. Many were in service. In the latter part of the 18th century there were the tailors, and a shoe maker and cordwainer. In the Victorian age there were two shops, two butchers, two carpenters, a wheelwright, a shoe maker, three bakers and a saddler.

There is a superb dovecote built c1600. In those days, doves were valued as a source of meat. An old mill which ground corn and was powered by the River Windrush, is situated at the east end of the village.

Naunton has a cricket team. There are social activities which include entertainment, in which many of the villagers are involved. Each April there is an event, and transport is provided if required, for the elderly to attend.

The Church
ST ANDREW

There is evidence of a church in Naunton dating back to Saxon times. A stone cross was unearthed from under the nave. Only the lower walls of the chancel, nave and tower, remain of the 12th century building. In the 15th and 16th centuries it was mainly rebuilt.

The tower is perpendicular and is around the same date. The stone pulpit is circa 1400 and stands on a modern plinth. The font is of the 15th century and has a modern step. There are two sundials on the tower. These originate from 1748. The south dial has an inscription 'Lux Umbra Dei' which means 'Light is the shadow of God'. The east window was inserted in Victorian times and the whole floor level was raised during 1899. New pews and choir seats were installed in 1978 and the door was replaced the same year.

On the opposite side of the road to the church, the Reverend Edward Litton lived in the rectory from 1860 to 1897. He was a friend of the author Charles Dodgson, who wrote 'Alice in Wonderland'. It is said that it was the Reverend Litton's daughter who inspired the author to write the story.

The Pub
BLACK HORSE INN

The Black Horse has been serving the local population ever since the 1870s. It was originally a row of tiny cottages. It has the proportions of a farm worker's home, with open log fires and flagstone floors. Electricity was at one time provided by a water wheel situated by the dovecote, which drove a generator. It was known for the supply to fail if a trout got stuck in the wheel.

Besides bar snacks, a full menu is available and the pub also offers Bed & Breakfast. Very popular with walkers, it is an ideal centre for circular walks in the area.

Sundial - St Andrews

The village pump - Naunton

Chapter 8

Ilmington - Warwickshire

◆ ◆ ◆

Ebrington - Gloucestershire

The Village
ILMINGTON . WARWICKSHIRE
situated near Mickleton and signposted off B4632
This is a large village, comprising of many Cotswold stone
houses, the village boasts two village greens

The Church
ST MARY THE VIRGIN

There is no direct road to the church. This is approached by footpaths, from the road that encircles the church. Lime trees line the path and these represent the Apostles. The embattled tower houses six bells, five of which are of the 17th century, the sixth added in 1921.

As you enter the porch, observe the de Montfort coat of arms. On approaching the doorway, three different periods of architecture can be seen. The arch over the door is 11th century Norman. This has a dogstooth carving, typical of the period. There is a canopied niche of decorated style c1300. This probably held a statue of the Virgin Mary until the Reformation, when it was destroyed. Underneath there is a Tudor arch, containing a stoop for holy water. The font is probably of the 14th century and the plinth on which it stands is of a later date.

In the nave there are two Norman windows in each of the

Statue of Joseph, Mary & Jesus - St Mary the Virgin

north and south walls, being the only sides, in the 14th century, where the clerestory was installed. The north transept was added in the 14th century and the south transept early in the 19th century. The carving in the north transept arch appears to be that of a Mongolian woman. On the opposite arch, the male and female heads are possibly of Zacharias and Elizabeth. On the south side of the arch there is a carving depicting Joseph and Mary.

The chancel arch is Norman. The carving of the sphinx-like head on the north of the pillar is Byzantine. The pillar on the other side has little or no carving. There is what appears to be a sedilia on each side of the chancel. The east window stone tracing is 1200-1300 and the glass is probably early 19th century. On the south side of the sanctuary there is a piscina and nearby there are three stone seats.

A striking and unusual feature of St Mary's is the superb oak woodwork. During the 1930s Robert Thomson, 'The Mouseman of Kilburn', supervised the carvings of a mouse which can be seen on doors, desk, pulpit and pews, also on the oak memorial plaque in memory of Spencer Flower, who played a leading role in the refurbishment. There are a number of interesting memorial tablets throughout the church.

Mouse carving - St Mary the Virgin

The Pub

in fact there are two

THE HOWARD ARMS

Has 17th century origins. It has been extensively and tastefully refurbished. Besides having a full menu available lunchtime and evening, overnight guests are catered for.

THE RED LION

This probably has 17th century origins, with flagstone floors and low beamed ceilings. It was originally thatched and adjoined a forge and stable, now disused. Bar snacks and a full menu is available.

◆ ◆ ◆

The Village
EBRINGTON . GLOUCESTERSHIRE
2 miles east of Chipping Campden off B4035
signposted just a short distance away

This charming village with its honey coloured cottages and houses, some thatched, enjoys splendid views of the surrounding countryside. It is known to those who live locally as 'Yubberton' and has a range of property dating from the 16th century to the present day. There are many different styles of building. Whilst the village is expanding a little, there is no longer a shop or post office, the nearest being at Chipping Campden.

As one of the venues for Morris dancing, Ebrington hosts a number of visits by the dance groups during the course of the year. It is claimed by some to be the home of the Cotswold Morris Men. A village fête and flower show is held and is well supported. The actor who once played Walter Gabriel in the radio serial 'The Archers' is said to have based the character on a villager here.

A number of notables have resided in the area, amongst these Sir John Fortescue. It was during the reign of Henry VI that Sir John bought one of the manors at Ebrington from the Corbet family. However, the property was taken away from him when he lost his civil rights during the reign of Edward IV and was exiled to Holland. Following the Battle of Tewkesbury he was once again in the King's favour. He returned to Ebrington and retired, where he died in 1476.

The Church
ST EADBURGHA

Built in stone and roofed in stone, St Eadburgha's has an embattled western tower with pinnacles, which houses six bells. On the south wall there is a sundial.

Upon entry to the south porch, on the west side there is a stone coffin which is thought to be from Saxon times. To the east side there is a window with a leper seat below. The window was to provide a view to the church for the afflicted, and as with the church interior, was subject to Victorian restoration. The doorway is of Norman origins and was similarly restored in the Victorian period.

Going into the church, on the south wall there is a commemoration tablet to the 'Ebrington Cow Charity'. This was a bequest made in 1632 by William Keyte. It makes interesting reading. There are other memorials to the Keyte family in the south transept. Also in the south transept there is a vandalised piscina. This would have been done by troops of the Roundhead army. In the chancel on the south wall are the busts of Sir John Keyte and his wife Margaret. Sir John died in 1662. The east window is modern and dates from 1964.

In the sanctuary on the north side stands the tomb of Sir John Fortescue, Lord Chancellor, which is early 16th century. The recumbent effigy depicts Sir John in the robes of the Lord Chancellor.

The oak pulpit has origins from the Stuart period. Restoration work has been carried out. The font steps are believed to be early English. During the Victorian restoration the church was re-pewed. However, some of the original pew ends are to be seen.

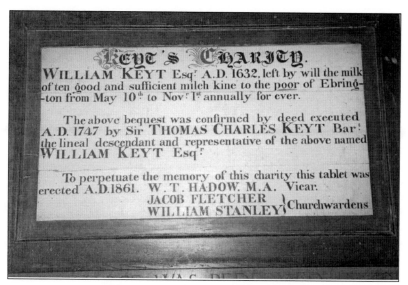

William Keyt's bequest - St Eadburgha

The Pub
THE EBRINGTON ARMS

This ancient building is one of the oldest in the village, with parts of its structure dating back 500 years. At one time, part of the present building was a butcher's. As a pub it started to sell beer and cider 300 yeas ago, and has held a full licence since 1722. Over the years alterations and extensions have taken place, but all has been done in such a manner as to retain its old-world charm.

Entering through a doorway which has a door original to when the building was erected, there are flagstone floors and beamed ceilings. The bar has an old log burning fireplace. In the restaurant a rack for bacon hanging is suspended from the ceiling, and there is another old fashioned fireplace.

'The Ebrington' is very much the centre of activities. It is in the Crib League, Dominoes and Darts. The cricketers meet here and Morris dancers visit. It caters for overnight guests, having two letting rooms. Bar snacks and a full menu are available. Outside is a patio garden area where meals and drinks are served. Lastly, observe The Ebrington Arms unique sign at the front of the building.

Part 3

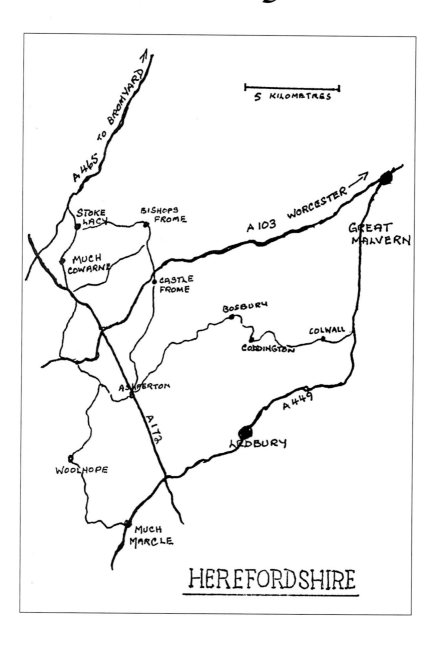

Chapter 9

Colwall - Herefordshire

◆ ◆ ◆

Coddington - Herefordshire

◆ ◆ ◆

Much Marcle - Herefordshire

The Village
COLWALL . HEREFORDSHIRE
situated NW of Ledbury and SW of Malvern
travelling from Malvern on A449 turn onto B4218
Colwall is signposted

Overlooked by the Malvern Hills, Colwall shows much evidence of its Victorian past with many houses of that age mingling with both modern and earlier dated property. There is a library with computer facilities. Shops include a grocer, a butcher and a post office.

A major employer in the area besides the hotels is Coca Cola Schweppes. This company operates a bottling plant for Malvern water which is piped from the Primeswell Spring. The spring is situated on the western slope of the Malvern Hills from an altitude of 230 metres and 1-8km from the village of Colwall. The company today makes no claims about magical curing powers of the water as the Victorians did. They did claim that Malvern Water was exceedingly pure water. Malvern water has been bottled for at least 350 years and the spring that supplies the factory has been in use since 250BC.

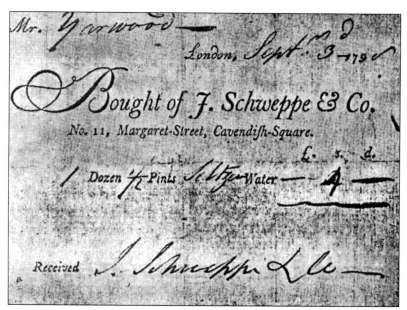

The oldest invoice of the house of Schweppes, September 3rd 1798

Malvern Hills & Springs

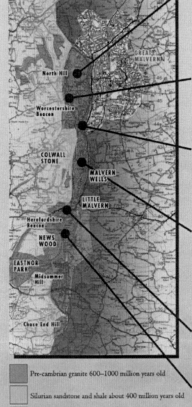

ST ANN'S WELL rises within the Malvern Hills 230 metres above sea level. The water was bottled first by Burrows then by Schweppes from the 1850's to the 1950's. The water rights are now possessed by the Malvern Hills Conservators for public use.

HAYSLAD rises on the western boundary fault 275m above sea level. Partially contained for the public water supply, the spout is a popular rendezvous for people to fill their own containers.

ROYAL WELL SPRING rises on the western boundary fault 275m above sea level. The source for the Royal Well Mineral Water Company which bottled water and soft drinks from 1870 to 1900, now derelict.

HOLYWELL rises at the head of a small valley 210m above sea level. The water was the first to be bottled with a record dating back to 1610–1620. Burrows, Schweppes, Cuffs and most recently, John Parkes has bottled the water since 1850.

PRIMESWELL SPRING rises on the thrust fault below the Herefordshire Beacon 230m above sea level. The source for Malvern Water today.

WALM'S WELL rises on the thrust fault below the Herefordshire Beacon 220m above sea level. Supplies the Eastnor Estate.

North Hill

GREAT MALVERN

Worcestershire Beacon

COLWALL STONE

MALVERN WELLS

LITTLE MALVERN

Herefordshire Beacon

NEWS WOOD

EASTNOR PARK

Midsummer Hill

Chase End Hill

Pre-cambrian granite 600–1000 million years old

Silurian sandstone and shale about 400 million years old

Triassic mudstone about 200 million years old

Map of springs in Malvern Hills

Nearby, Malvern developed into a spa town and it became fashionable for visitors to 'take the waters', or 'take the cure', and to take bracing walks on the hills. The therapeutic cures reached a peak in the Victorian era. The bottling plant in Colwall was built in 1892.

It was granted a Royal Warrant by Princess Mary Adelaide in 1895, and by King George V in 1911. It is supplier to the present Queen Elizabeth II. In 2001 the factory was visited by HRH Princess Anne.

It is interesting to note that in 1987, seven million litres were bottled. By 1990 this had increased to 21 million litres.

In the village there is a cricket club, including a ladies' team. There are private schools, one of which is The Downs, which opened in 1900. In 1932 the poet WH Auden taught English in the school. Elizabeth Browning lived in the vicinity, residing at Hope End, before moving to Wimpole Street. The house was situated some two miles southwest of the church, but burned down in 1910.

The railway station was built in 1860. The Colwall Park Hotel was built in 1903 and opened in 1905, in order to accommodate those attending the local racecourse which existed at that time.

Water Company works - Colwall

The Church
ST JAMES THE GREAT

The church is situated a little over a mile from the village centre. It was as a result of the railway arriving in the area that the village developed away from the immediate vicinity of the church, and a community quickly built up. Visitors wishing to visit the church should proceed to the lower part of the village where the church is signposted.

The tower, which is embattled, was built in the 14th century up to its second stage, which was added at a later date. The niche on the east side once held a calvary or pieta, the Virgin Mary with the dead body of Christ in her lap. Until the millennium the tower housed eight bells, but as a result of a renovation project the number was increased to ten.

The south porch is 16th century and the south door is Norman. The south aisle is 13th century. The roof was restored in 1675 and the north aisle added in 1880. It was built to increase the seating capacity in general, but specifically for the children of Walwyn's Grammar School. The pews are marked in red paint 'Grocer's School' and were given by Humphry Walwyn. He was

Tile - St James The Great, Colwall

a member of the Worshipful Company of Grocers. In 1614 he funded the Free Grammar School in Colwall, leaving a legacy for maintenance. The school is now known as The Elms School.

On the north wall an ancient tile can be seen. It is of the late 13th century and depicts a man digging. It is one of a series of twelve covering the months of the year. In this case the month is March. The chancel was built in 1865-6 and replaced a Norman one. In the sanctuary the reredos is a carving of a lamb flanked by an angel on each side. On the south wall of the sanctuary there are the remains of a shelved piscina. On the east wall a memorial coat of arms in stone can be observed. This is dated 1587 and is to the parents of Humphry Walwyn.

The pulpit is Jacobean and has a back panel and tester. Affixed to the south wall is a brass tablet to the memory of Elizabeth Harford, who died in 1590 and is depicted with her husband, who is dressed in armour. Six sons and four daughters are also shown. The font is 13th century and the wooden cover is dated 1938. Carvings on the half pillar in the west wall depict a female figure with raised arms. This is believed to be a fertility symbol.

Outside the churchyard there are the remains of what appears to be an ancient cross and by the east gate stands a timbered building. This was what was the church ale house and is dated 1530. In the middle of the 17th century it was converted into almshouses but was last used as such in 1930. In 1989 it was restored and its use changed to that of the church hall.

The Pub

there are three

THE CHASE INN

Situated in Upper Colwall, the inn was first licensed in 1860. It overlooks Colwall village and the surrounding countryside and has superb views. There is a garden patio. Bar snacks are served at lunchtimes, but not on Tuesday and Sunday.

THE CROWN

A Victorian building which has been extensively refurbished. Bar snacks are served and a full menu available. The landlord is proud of the real ales served.

THE YEW TREE

This is the oldest of the Colwall pubs and is of the 16th/17th century. It is typical of that period, with flagstone floors and beams.

◆ ◆ ◆

The Village
CODDINGTON . HEREFORDSHIRE
situated approx 5 miles SW of Malvern
take B4237 from Malvern then B4218 to Colwall
Coddington is then signposted

Surrounded by farmland and orchards, Coddington has superb views of the Malvern Hills. It is a village of few houses, some of which date back to the 16th and 17th centuries. The population is only about 120.

At one time a school that provided for children of servicemen serving in India was established in the village. Amongst its pupils, Michael Bentine well known for his TV and radio fame, Jeremy Thorpe the former Liberal Party Leader, and Sarah Churchill the niece of Sir Winston Churchill, may be noted. The school closed in 1957.

Within the village is the Coddington Vineyard. This was once an apple orchard. Dennis and Ann Savage replaced the trees with vines in 1985, and had the first crop of grapes in 1989. There are 3000 vines planted on two acres of land, which produce

Time for pruning at Coddington Vineyard,
Ann Savage (prop.) at work

3000 litres, or 4000 standard bottles, of wine. Three varieties of grapes are grown, Bacchus, Ortega and Pinot Gris. The wines are produced on the estate and have won many awards. They are recognised as being typical of English wines.

The vineyard is open to visitors March-December 2-5pm daily, with the exception of Tuesday and Wednesday. It is, however, possible to make other arrangements by telephone. In one of the outbuildings close to the fine 17th century farmhouse, there is a shop containing an old cider mill, where wines and pottery can be purchased. All this is set in beautiful surrounds of gardens and a small lake.

The Church
ALL SAINTS

Built of stone, it has a western tower and spire, which houses six bells, soon to be renovated, thanks to a Lottery grant and the hard work of local supporters. The building is of the 12th century, on the site of an earlier Saxon church. There have been a number of reconstructions and renovations. All Saints consists of a nave and chancel.

Upon entry into the church through the south door it can be seen that much restoration was undergone in the Victorian era, the restoration being carried out as sympathetically as possible, with the Norman features being retained. It was also re-pewed, the old box pews and pulpit being removed. The 1866 restoration was at a cost of approximately £2000, paid for by Mrs Hope of Malvern. She was the sister-in-law of the Rev Edward Higgins of Bosbury Manor. Included in this restoration, the nave roof was repaired with best English oak and the walls of the eastern half of the nave was dismantled and rebuilt with the same stones.

On the north west wall there is a war memorial tablet. The chancel arch is 13th century. In this area the roof was renewed. An organ chamber and vestry were added to the north side. The reredos consists of round intersecting arcades, supported by polished marble pillars. Two 13th century east windows contain stained glass which was installed in 1908 to the memory of Kathleen Bulkley, who died in 1907. A piscina can be seen in the south side. A 13th/14th century pulpit window with fragments of mediaeval glass overlooks the Victorian pulpit. The original 13th century font bowl was damaged and a replacement bowl put into position.

Outside in the churchyard stands an ancient preaching cross, where the priest could deliver his orations. It consists of five steps with a chamfered base. During the Civil War it was vandalised by Puritan troops. Restoration work was carried out during Victorian times and the replacement cross added.

What is believe to be a Saxon burial was discovered in recent years near the south wall. It was decided to leave this undisturbed. Near the east wall of the church stands the tomb of Rev Edward Kerie Lovell, who was the rector of Coddington 1848-1860. His son Edward is buried in the same tomb. He was a friend of TE Lawrence, who visited the village from time to time.

The Pub

There is no pub in Coddington now, although there were once two, the Golden Cross and The Plough, which was also a shop. The nearest pub is **The Farmer's Arms** at Wellington Heath, a short distance away. The Farmer's Arms was once an old farmhouse and originates from the Tudor period. Once a cider house, it has been extended and modernised over the years. The bar area has oak beams. An outdoor terrace overlooking Frith Wood adds to the attractions. A full menu is available with daily specials. A children's play area is a further facility.

◆ ◆ ◆

The Village
MUCH MARCLE . HEREFORDSHIRE
situated on A449 Ledbury-Ross on Wye road 5 miles SW of
Ledbury

The village is surrounded by fruit growing and farming land. It
consists of houses that date back to the 16th century and various
periods up to the present date. Local facilities include a shop that is
a post office, an Off Licence and stores. A memorial hall was built
in 1921 to the memory of those who died in the Great War.

In 1571 an amazing landslip occurred on 17 February at 6pm.
Marcle Hill started to move and it continued to do so for three
days. During this time it made a loud roaring noise. A whole
twenty acre field moved to a higher level and left a chasm that
was 40ft deep, 520ft long and 400ft wide. It destroyed the chapel
of Kynaston. The chapel bell was dug up some years later. Many
cattle were killed in this disaster, which became known as 'The
Wonder'.

It is not possible to write about Much Marcle without
mentioning Weston Cider. This old established family business
really started when Henry Weston came to farm at The Bounds

Oak barrels - Weston Cider, Much Marcle

Alter frontals by William Morris - All Saints, Coddington

Shire horses - Weston Cider , Much Marcle

in 1878. He was aged 28. The Bounds is a farmhouse which dates back to the early 17th century. Continuing the tradition of using fruit from the farm orchards to make cider and perry, was very much part of the way of life in rural communities. It was the custom to have cider in the cellar for the family, and a hogshead was made available for workers to have their wooden 'costrels' filled for their daily ration.

At that time Henry was a tenant farmer, and being an astute man, he could foresee a threat from overseas imports, which were increasing due to the expanding British Empire. He then made the decision to put his cider making practice onto a commercial basis. With the high quality of the product and much hard work, customers were gained and their numbers progressively increased. So much so, that now, as well as a healthy home market, the company exports to thirteen countries worldwide, something that Henry would have been very proud of, particularly that it remains a family business.

Oak vats are used to mature the cider, some of the vats being nearly 200 years old. Interestingly, three of the vats are named, Gloucester, Worcester, and Hereford. These are the counties covered by this book.

Cider Vats - Hereford, Gloucester & Worcester

Henry Weston and Children with Apples

At Weston's, visitors have the opportunity to tour the mill. There is a museum and a shop where samples can be tasted. There is also a variety of gifts on sale. Refreshments can be purchased in the Visitor's Centre and full meals can be obtained at The Scrumpy House Restaurant and Bar. The Edwardian Garden was opened in the summer of 2003 by HRH Prince Philip Duke of Edinburgh, who took the opportunity to take the reins of the dray pulled by the shire horses. Visitors can have a ride on the dray, which takes them through the village and is a popular attraction. In the enclosure adjoining the car park there are rare breeds of cattle on show.

Hellens, another point of interest in the village, is an historic fortified house that dates back to mediaeval times. It is reputed to have a ghost and a secret passage. It has a fascinating history and is worth a visit. Opening days are confined to Wednesday, Saturday, Sunday, Bank Holidays and by special arrangement.

The Church
ST BARTHOLOMEW

Built of stone in the 13th century, it has a central tower, which is embattled and houses six bells. It has a clock on the east face, and gargoyles on the north and south faces. Entry is through the south door, whereupon it will be seen that the church was re-pewed in Victorian times.

On the north side of the nave, visitors will immediately see an effigy carved in oak. It is believed to be that of Walter de Helyon, who it is also believed lived at Hellens. It is of the 14th century. He was buried at Asperton. The memorial was probably erected by his only child Joanna. By the organ there is a brass plaque. This has an etching of a child playing an instrument, with an angel looking on.

Situated in the chancel is the Grandison tomb 1360-1370. This contains the remains of Blanche Mortimer, who was the daughter of Roger Mortimer, first Earl of March. The chapel contains a 14th century tomb with effigies of a knight and lady, the knight being in armour and the lady in a gown. Neither identity is known. The second tomb is the Kyrle tomb and is of the 16th century, of black and white marble. It features a lady in a dress and a man in armour. There are hedgehog and claw carvings at their feet.

The east window has stained glass and the reredos is of inlaid brass. The door to the missing rood loft can be seen. The remains of a piscina exist in the south aisle. With origins of the 12th century, the font has a wooden cover which was added in 1975.

Outside in the churchyard, the preaching cross is c15th century. The yew tree is extremely old. Various dates are claimed, ranging from 1,000-1,500yrs. The hollow trunk has seats inside and can hold 10-12 people. Due to the branches sagging, supports had to be placed under them. These are old gas lamp posts, which were obtained from the Cheltenham authorities. Also in the churchyard are a number of tabletop tombs.

The Pub

there are three

THE SLIP TAVERN
once known as The New Inn

Once a cider house, it has been altered and extended over the years. The Slip serves bar snacks, has a full menu and is well known for its varied menu with an international flavour. Folk evenings are held regularly. There is a garden area with seating and tables.

THE ROYAL OAK INN

The inn was built c1830 and has been extended considerably over the years. Bar snacks are served and a full menu is available. There is a function room and a skittle alley.

WALWYN ARMS

The oldest of the village pubs, it dates back to the 17th century. It has changed its name a number of times. In 1797 it was known as The Ship and Castle. It has also been known as Baker's. In the 19th century William Robinson sold the inn to Edward Walwyn from Hellens. The pub then took on the name of the family.

At one time the building had a butcher's shop and slaughter house attached. Meetings of the Ross and Archenfield branch of the Girls' Friendly Society took place at The Walwyn. In the 1900s it was a popular venue for touring cyclists.

There is a skittle alley and pool table. Besides serving bar snacks, a full menu is available.

◆ ◆ ◆

Chapter 10

Bosbury - Herefordshire

♦ ♦ ♦

Castle Frome - Herefordshire

♦ ♦ ♦

Bishops Frome - Herefordshire

♦ ♦ ♦

Ashperton - Herefordshire

The Village
BOSBURY . HEREFORDSHIRE
situated on B4220
take B4212 road from Ledbury
then turn onto B4220 which leads directly into village

Surrounded by orchards and farming land, Bosbury is rich in 16th century buildings. This village was once much larger and was considered to be a place of significance. It had a bishop's palace, belonging to the bishops of Hereford. This is now Old Courts Farm. Nearby, the Knights Templar had a preceptory at Temple Court. The ancient grammar school c1600 is now the Church Hall.

At the edge of the village stood a Gospel Yew, where a clergyman delivered a sermon daily. A well named Job's Well attracted people to take its waters, as it was believed to cure eye problems. Prince Rupert's army stayed in the village at the time of the Civil War.

In past times 29th May was a day of note and was celebrated here more than May Day, the reason being that this was when indoor servants and lady's maids could change their employment.

The Church
THE HOLY TRINITY

This building has 12th century origins and evidence shows that it was built on the site of an earlier Saxon church. The tower, which is free standing from the church, is embattled and was built in the first part of the 13th century. This large structure with walls 6ft thick was, apart from its present use as a bell tower, probably built as a refuge during the raids from the Welsh. It houses six bells. On approaching the church a preaching cross stands. This type of cross is typical of the 14th century.

Upon entry into the south porch, the doorway is 12th century and the frame of the porch is 15th century. The remains of a stoup can be seen. This was destroyed by the troops of the Parliamentary Army during the Civil War. Going into the church, which consists of a nave, chancel, north aisle and south aisle, the font is situated in the south aisle and is believed to be some 800 years old. During the course of renovation in 1844 it was discovered that an earlier font from probably Saxon times was situated underneath in an upside down position. This crude Saxon bowl is now on display in the north aisle.

In 1921 a fire destroyed part of the roof of the south aisle and the nave. The window in this area is modern. The west wall of the nave is the oldest part of the church and is dated 12th century, with the aisles, the arcade and celestory being added in the late 12th century. Transitional in style, the scallop capitals are Norman and the pointed arches early English.

Most of the stained glass windows were destroyed during the Civil War by troops of the Parliamentary Army. There are, however, attractive windows of modern times. A memorial window to the memory of Marian Buck of Noverings 1909-1947 is situated in the north wall. She was a local benefactor.

Bishop of Hereford 1282-1316 - Holy Trinity Church, Bosbury

The pulpit is basically Jacobean but has been restored and altered. The carved panels are thought to be Flemish of the late 16th century and represent the Adoration of the Magi, the Agony in the Garden, the Crucifixion and the Flight into Egypt. The lectern is Jacobean.

The chancel arch is of a little later date than the nave, with slender columns, and is partly moulded. A fine example of 15th century carving is displayed in the screen, with a vine decoration. The panelling in the lower part of the screen is to the memory of novelist Edna Lyall, Ada Ellen Bayly d1903. She was the sister of the vicar at that time.

Upon entering the chancel, memorials to the Harford family will be seen. On the north wall is a memorial to Richard Harford d1578 and his wife Martha d1601. On the south wall is a memorial to his father John Harford d1559. The east window commemorates the family of Rev Edward Higgins, who lived for over fifty years at Bosbury House. Re-entering the south aisle a damaged memorial stone, uncovered in 1776, to Stephen Swinefield d1282, is on the south wall. It was placed at the church by his son Richard de Swinefield, who was Bishop of Hereford 1282-1316. The carved head beneath is believed to portray the bishop. Nearby two large slabs indicate the burials of two Knights Templar from 13th century.

Re-pewing of the church took place in Victorian times.

The Pub
THE BELL INN

This one time coaching inn was built in the 16th century. It is beamed and has flagstone floors underneath the carpeting. As with many coaching houses, The Bell once had a smithy and stabling for horses. At present its sporting connections mean a busy time during every season. There is a cricket team, a football team and a pool team.

Light refreshments are available in the evening on Friday/Saturday, and at lunchtime on Sunday.

In years past, several local inns were closed, The Crown, The Brook, The Old Country and The Dog.

The Village
CASTLE FROME . HEREFORDSHIRE
situated on B4214 Ledbury-Bromyard road 6 miles from
Ledbury

The village in this case is tiny and consists of only a few houses
and farms. As its name indicates, there was once a castle, although
little evidence of this now exists.

Castle Frome is known for its connections with the Mormon
Church. This was brought about by the farmer John Benbow,
who lived at Hill Farm. In 1840 he joined the Latter Day Saints
and went to live in Salt Lake City USA, taking with him other
converts. The pond near Hill House has been used for baptisms
for many years and Mormon pilgrims still come from USA to see
the pond and be baptised.

The Church
ST MICHAEL

Built of stone and mainly Norman, it was restored in the Victorian
era, with the porch and bell turret being added at that time. The
turret houses three mediaeval bells. Entry is through the south
door. The tympanum is plain.

Immediately on going through the door you are confronted
by a magnificent font, dated c1170. The detail is worth studying.
It depicts the Baptism of Christ. The font stands upon three
crouching figures, of which two have their heads missing. The
font is a remarkable piece of craftsmanship.

The church consists of a nave and chancel. The walls were once
plastered but this has been removed. The nave ceiling beams are
of the 15th century and the pulpit 17th century. The altar rails
originate from the 18th century.

By the north wall of the chancel stands a tomb with recumbent
effigies. This is known as the 'Unett Tomb'. It depicts a cavalier,
his wife and children. Interestingly, there is a drawing dated 1817
hanging on the wall above. This is of the tomb and shows the lady
to be lying on the left of the man. This is opposite to their present
positions.

What may have been a piscina is in the south wall, but it is now obscured by mediaeval tiles. In the nearby window there is a small stone carving of a crusader holding a heart. It was customary, if a crusader died abroad, that his heart be brought home for burial.

A booklet entitled 'Castle Frome' is available in the church. It is inexpensive and contains superb photographs. Purchasing this gives support to this lovely church.

The Pub

Although there is no pub in the village, there are a few in the locality. In the nearby village of Bishop's Frome, at the village centre, there are two, **The Chase Inn** and **The Green Dragon.** A little further afield there are **The Major's Arms**, **The Fir Tree** and **The Five Bridges**.

The font - St Michaels, Castle Frome

The Village
BISHOP'S FROME . HEREFORDSHIRE
situated on B4214 Ledbury-Bromyard road

Surrounded by fruit and hop growing, the village has a mixture of building styles and ages, from 17th century through Victorian to the present day. Facilities within the village include a post office and stores, a hairdresser's and a garage. There is a Community Centre which is very much the focus of the many events that take place. The Hop Pocket Craft Centre is situated just a short distance from the village, near the junction of the B4214 with the A4103, and is signposted.

The Hop Pocket was originally a farm which diversified in 1988, and is an ideal place for gifts. On site there is a small Garden Centre, and a Jeweller's where designer jewellery can be purchased and made to your own requirements. In the same unit, fashion clothes can be purchased or made as required. A Delicatessen has a fine selection of game, meats, preserves, oils, etc. There is a Wine Shop offering a selection of wines, spirits and a variety of fruit juices. There is a florist and designer handbags, antiques and embroidery materials are available too. The Hop Pocket also has a Restaurant, where freshly cooked food can be obtained. Amidst all of these things, a host of gifts is available, which includes ceramics, prints, toys and local history/guide books. Disabled and baby changing facilities are within the main building, and there is ample car parking.

The Church
ST MARY THE VIRGIN

Almost certainly situated on the site of an earlier Saxon church, St Mary's is built of stone. It has an embattled tower which houses six bells. It was built in two stages, the lower part dated c1340 and the upper part added later. The bells and frame on which they are hung were installed in 1975, replacing an earlier ring of six that had not been in use since Victorian times. The replacement bells came from the redundant church of St Lawrence at Burwarton, Shropshire. The old Sanctus Bell has been renovated and is in use for the weekday services. The tower also houses a clock dated c1842.

Entry through the south porch, which is of the 19th century, takes you to a superb Norman doorway, which has plain shafts and leafy capitals. The arch itself is carved in a bold Chevron design. The south wall of the nave is 12th century, as is the north wall.

The ancient font is of Norman origins c1160. It stands on a plinth of later date. Its plain bowl and lead lining is unusual. There are only about twenty in the whole country. On the north wall the clappers of the old bells are on display, and the old parish chest stands near the centre of the nave. It dates from the 16th/17th century, is made of oak and has iron straps. One of the original three locks is missing.

To the north side of the church is the Lady Chapel, added in 1861. The arcade which separates it from the nave, although built in the Norman style, is of the same date. On the east wall a memorial to Margery, daughter of John Pychard of Paunton Court, and to her husband George de la Downes 1598, is sited. A smaller chapel was formed in 1994 and has been for weekday use and for private devotion. At the rear of the organ, a large painting is to be seen. It was the work of a former vicar and depicts Christ on the Cross.

The chancel arch is of the late 12th century and has a zig-zag decoration. The chancel screen is of mainly 15th century origins and was renovated in the 19th century. Old tombstones line the lower part of the wall in the chancel. The communion rails were made by a parishioner and gifted in 1994. The altar table is of the 17th century and stands to the front of the 19th century altar.

Three east windows in 19th century stained glass depict scenes of the Birth, Baptism, Transfiguration, Crucifixion and Ascension of Christ. On the east end of the south wall there is a piscina. Upon re-entry into the nave, the pulpit stands near the south wall. The wall behind the pulpit contains another piscina, which indicates that an altar once stood near here. The recess a little further to the west of the pulpit, that is ornamented with ballflowers, contains the effigy of The Crusader. His habit is that of a Knight Templar. It is thought that he could be of the local landowners, the Devereux family.

Returning to the south door, the old key of the church is displayed above. Outside in the churchyard there are the remains of an old preaching cross.

The Pub

there are two at the village centre

THE CHASE INN

Built in 1860 for the purpose of providing for the many hop pickers during the season, it has been refurbished a number of times over the years and now offers holiday and overnight accommodation. Bar snacks are served and a full menu is available.

As a matter of interest, a sign above the bar refers to Weston's Old Rosie Vintage Cider at 9d per gallon and Uncle Tom's Best at ½d per gallon. These are of course 1860 prices.

The building contains an old well but this is now covered. At one time a slaughter house adjoined The Chase and provided the meat for the butchers, then nearby.

THE GREEN DRAGON

This is a 17th century building with beamed ceilings and a flagstone floor.

At one time the area in and around the village boasted seven pubs, of which five remain, the two already mentioned, plus **The Major Arms**, **The Fir Tree Inn** and **The Five Bridges**, which are nearby. **The Wheatsheaf Inn** and **The Holly Tree** closed.

◆ ◆ ◆

The Village
ASHPERTON . HEREFORDSHIRE
situated 5 miles NW of Ledbury on A417

Amid farming and fruit growing, the small village of Ashperton has quite a mixture of styles and ages of properties, which covers the period of the 16th/17th century up to the present day.

Ashperton was at one time the property of John de Monmouth. This ended with his death in 1270. The land was then inherited by William de Grandison. By 1292 William had built a manor at Ashperton and it was in that year that he received permission from the King to crenellate and convert it into a castle. In 1327 William's son John de Grandison, who was the great nephew of Bishop Cantilupe St Thomas of Hereford, was made Bishop of Exeter.

Little evidence of the castle remains today. Only a mount encircled by what was the moat.

The Church
ST BARTHOLOMEW

Built in local stone, the church has 13th century origins, but was entirely rebuilt in the 14th century. It was here that John de Grandison, who became Bishop of Exeter 1327-1369, was baptised, as was his sister Katherine Lady Montacute, wife of the first Earl of Salisbury. John and Katherine were both born in the nearby castle.

Built in a cruciform structure, a number of renovations have taken place. The tower formerly occupied a central position. This was altered to the western end and was rebuilt in that ;position in 1849, using stone from the castle. The bells, which consist of a peal of four, were re-hung. A further restoration took place 1992/93 but the bells are now only chimed, as it is not considered safe enough to stand the vibrations of a full peal.

Upon entering the church through the south porch, a Victorian font will be observed. The original font is situated near the chancel and is thought to date from the 13th century. It was discovered in the churchyard. On the west wall, a balcony can be seen. On this stands a small organ case. It is probably early 19th century and may have housed a type of barrel organ, much in use during that period. Unfortunately the works are missing.

The nave roof is in flat barrel form and is sealed. It has five late 16th century moulded tie beams with plastered trusses. Approaching the north transept on the east wall there is a piscina. The chancel roof is the same construction as that in the nave, but has moulded tie beams which are of the same date. The reredos in the sanctuary is in carved stone and depicts the Crucifixion with angels above. A piscina can be observed in the south wall.

In the chancel is a colourful display of kneelers. These were made by a group of ladies and took some ten years to complete. They illustrate the history of the village from Roman times to beyond 2000. They are superbly done and are a pleasure to look at.

Outside in the churchyard twelve yews line the footpath, as was the custom, and represent the Twelve Disciples. On the south transept there is a sundial. On the south side of the tower there is an external staircase.

Barrel Organ - St Bartholomew's, Ashperton

The Pub
THE HOPTON ARMS

Originally used as an abattoir and as a bakery, parts of the pub are about 300 years old. The Hopton Arms is named after Colonel Hopton of nearby Canon Frame Court, a wealthy landowner. The colonel, who was a shooting enthusiast, acquired the property, extended it and converted it into a shooting lodge. Nowadays, following restoration, an authentic Victorian atmosphere has been created. This has been done by using the original fireplaces, beams, doors and windows, together with pictures which had been hidden away, now hanging on the wood panel walls.

There is a restaurant which offers an extensive menu and bar meals can be obtained. Overnight accommodation is available in a converted coach house, which has eleven en-suite rooms. As The Hopton Arms is set in two and a half acres of ground, there is ample room for a fenced off play area for children. Beyond the pub, there is a two acre field which has facilities for caravans and campers.

◆ ◆ ◆

Chapter 11

Much Cowarne - Herefordshire

♦ ♦ ♦

Stoke Lacy - Herefordshire

♦ ♦ ♦

Woolhope - Herefordshire

The Village
MUCH COWARNE . HEREFORDSHIRE
situated off A4103 Worcester-Hereford road

This scattered and well spread village is set in a farming, fruit and hop growing area. It consists of properties dating back to the 16th/17th centuries, and later buildings, timber framed, plus those of the present day conventional styles.

It was in the 13th century that Much Cowarne was granted a charter to hold a market and fair, such was the size and importance of the area. In times past, a large amount of hops was grown and the region attracted many itinerant workers. It was during the hop picking season that they would set up different venues to stage Bare Knuckle Fights.

The Church
ST MARY THE VIRGIN

To reach the church, follow the signposted road from the A4103. This road is narrow and twisting. Continue along for about 1½ miles. The church stands close to farm buildings.

Built of stone, it is mediaeval and has an embattled western tower, which houses six bells and is dated Norman to early English. At one time it had a spire. This was struck and destroyed by lightening in 1840 and was never rebuilt.

Before entering the church, visitors should walk around the outside to the north side. Here evidence can be seen of the demolition of what was the north aisle. The filled-in arcades are clearly visible. This was probably done in the 16th century. Approaching the south door, the remains of an ancient preaching cross are to be seen. The cross is of 14th/15th century origin.

Upon entry into the south aisle through the south door, the tomb of Edmund Fox of Leighton Court will immediately be seen. It has the recumbent effigies of Edmund and his wife Ann. Edmund was the son of Charles Fox, who was the Secretary at the Council Held In The Marches in the latter part of the 16th century. Their ten children are depicted on the side of the tomb and what appear to be three babies in a cot at the foot.

Nearby lies the badly mutilated recumbent figure of

Grimbaldus Pouncefot. It shows him in armour with his legs crossed. It is believed that his wife once lay beside him, but her whereabouts now seem to be unknown. According to legend, Grimbaldus was held prisoner in Tunis and a ransom demanded, this being 'a joint of his wife'. She cut off her hand to save him. An artist's impression of Constance, minus her hand and wrist, with Grimbaldus, is on display.

There is a piscina situated in the east wall of the south aisle and another in the south wall. In the chancel close to the sanctuary on the south side stands the monument to Sybil Reed and her four children, which was erected by her husband William. On the south wall of the sanctuary there is another piscina. The communion table is of the 17th century. To the north of the chancel is the vestry, which is of the 13th/14th century, as is the chancel itself.

The pulpit, font and pitch-pine pews are of the Victorian era.

The Pub

there are two which both stand on A4103

THE FIVE BRIDGES

This is just outside the fringe of the village. It was built in 1580 and was nearly destroyed in 1645 during the Cromwellian period. It was rebuilt in 1760 and was used as a coaching inn. It is classified as a Grade II listed building. Over the years the premises have been much extended, but the lounge bar retains its original ceiling beams. The name Five Bridges is derived from having to cross from the inn to Bishop's Frome.

During lunchtime sandwiches and salads and a Five Bridges Platter can be obtained. In the evening cooked meals are available. Fresh produce can also be purchased.

THE FIR TREE INN

This is a modernised 16th century inn. It has been a smithy and a blacksmith's dwelling in the 19th century. In the 1920s it was licensed to sell ale and cider. It was a venue for bare knuckle fighting, and during the hop picking season many of the hop pickers would drink here, but they had to provide their own drinking vessels, a jar or mug.

Nowadays, besides serving bar meals, there is a full menu available. The Fir Tree also has conference facilities, and caters for wedding receptions and dances. Besides this, static caravans are sited in the adjoining orchard, where it is possible to enjoy a relaxing holiday. There is a fishing lake and daily permits are obtainable.

◆ ◆ ◆

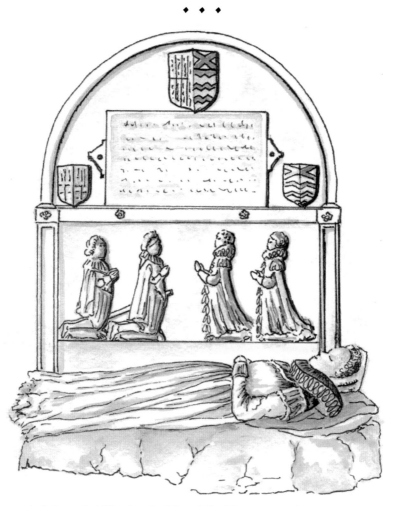

Memorial Tomb - St Mary The Virgin, Much Cowarne

The Village
STOKE LACY . HEREFORDSHIRE
situated approx 4 miles from Bromyard
straddled along A465 Bromyard-Hereford road

The properties in the village are quite scattered. A number of large houses, farms, cottages and oast conversions make up the village, housing little more than 250 people. Once mainly a hop growing area, it is now largely farming and orchards.

Electricity was not brought to Stoke Lacy until the mid-late 50s. In fact until then, most houses were lit by quite a variety of means, oil, paraffin, liquid gas and generators. Mains water was not available until 1971/73. Prior to that time the source of water was from springs.

Residents of Stoke Lacy are very active in the support of the village and have held many events to promote and preserve the well being of the community.

During the war, as a child, the late Adam Faith pop singer and actor, lived here. He was then known as Terence Nelhams.

There are connections with the Morgan Motor Company of Malvern. These originate from when the son of the Rev HG Morgan, who was in Stoke Lacy from 1887-1937, built and designed the prototype of the Morgan Motorcar in what is now known as The Old Rectory. The Morgan family continue to have close links with the village.

The Church
ST PETER AND ST PAUL

This is part of the amalgamation of parishes which took place in 1978. This includes Moreton Jefferies, now redundant but preserved by the Redundant Churches Trust, Much Cowarne, Ocle Pychard and Ullingswick.

Upon approaching the church, which has Norman origins, connections with the Morgan family will immediately be seen. The Morgan family graves are to the side of the footpath. Built of stone, St Peter and St Paul's has a western tower which houses six bells.

Entry is gained through the south porch. In the west wall of the porch is a stained glass memorial window, which is dedicated 'To the memory of John and Bridget Leavens of California USA and to all those who experienced the love and friendship engendered by the Morgan car, pray that we meet merrily in heaven'.

Upon going into the church, which consists of a nave and chancel, the full extent of the Victorian restoration can be seen. On the south wall, a list of incumbents is displayed and includes the prebendary Henry Morgan, who was the rector for 50 years. Previously he had acted as curate to his father.

The pews were part of the Victorian restoration and the windows in the nave are modern. The chancel arch is of Norman origin and has been restored. The 16th century oak screen is quite attractive but is not original to the church, and has been brought in from elsewhere. The choir stalls are of the late 19th century, but contain wood from the original stalls.

In the sanctuary in the south wall a piscina is to be seen. This is Victorian and is decorative with small polished marble pillars. The pulpit is constructed of stone and is of the same era. About the church there are a number of plaques. These include a memorial plaque to those killed in two World Wars.

The Pub
THE PLOUGH INN

This is situated on the A465 on the brow of the hill. It was once a blacksmith's shop and became a pub in 1905, at that time being just an ale and cider house. Since then a full licence has been granted.

Over the years the building has been altered and extended, but some of the original beams can be seen. Next door to The Plough is a cider mill that once belonged to the WW Symonds family. This supplied The Plough. However, after changes in ownership, the cider mill now belongs to the Wye Valley Breweries.

The Plough serves bar snacks and has a full menu available. There is a function room and a room with a pool table.

The Village
WOOLHOPE . HEREFORDSHIRE
situated 7 miles from Ledbury
reached by taking A449 from Ledbury
Woolhope is signposted at Much Marcle

The village is reached via narrow and winding lanes, the surrounding countryside being farming and orchards. Houses and farms date back many years. This is reflected in the amount of black and white timber framed buildings, some of which have 14th/15th century origins. The name Woolhope is pronounced 'Woolup' by locals.

The well known Booker family have long standing connections with the area. The one time shipping line owners are now the cash and carry company.

Opposite the church stands The Old Rectory. This 17th century building is now privately owned.

The Church
ST GEORGE'S

Upon entering the churchyard through the lychgate c1581, to the left of the footpath are remains of Gammonds Shop, which was believed to have been a carpenter's and coffin maker's workshop. Also on the left there are many unmarked graves. These are gypsy graves. It was one of their traditional burial places. To the right of the path stands a preaching cross, which was vandalised in 1548 by Puritans. It was restored in 1897 to commemorate Queen Victoria's Diamond Jubilee. The broken shaft was salvaged and has been placed to the rear of the church with a sundial on top.

At one time a wall encircled the churchyard. This was built by local farmers and they were required to maintain it, each having his own section. The wall no longer encircles the churchyard but it still stands on the left, which is to the west of the church. As it was built in sections, each section was only butted together and not interlocked. The farmers' duty to maintain the wall is listed in a document dated 1740 and held in the county record office.

The church has Norman origins and was built on the site of a wooden Saxon church, which burned down. Built in the 12th

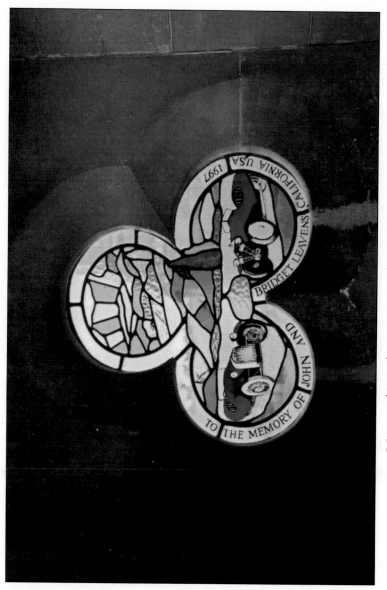

Memorial Window - St Peter & St Paul, Stoke Lacy

Godiva window - St George's Woolhope

century of stone, St George's has a western tower with a weather vane, which houses six bells and what is thought to be a Sanctus Bell. The tower is largely of the 13th century. There is evidence on the outside of the wall of a blocked doorway to the tower. It is said that the vicar of the time had the doorway blocked up, to make the bell ringers remain for the services.

As you enter the church, note the small crusader crosses etched into the stonework to the right of the door. An almost complete restoration of the church was done in Victorian times and is very evident, but this was sympathetically carried out. St George's consists of a nave, chancel, north aisle, vestry and south aisle. The nave was modified in the 13th century and the north aisle was added.

In the north wall a stained glass window is in memory of Arthur Dudley Stallard barrister at law, and of his wife Emblyn Eliza. The window depicts sisters Wulvia and Godiva, Lady Godiva of Coventry. The Manor of Woolhope was given to Hereford Cathedral by the sisters. Also on the north wall two ornate coffin lids can be seen. The date of these is uncertain, but they are thought to be Saxon.

The north aisle has origins in the early Norman period. It was

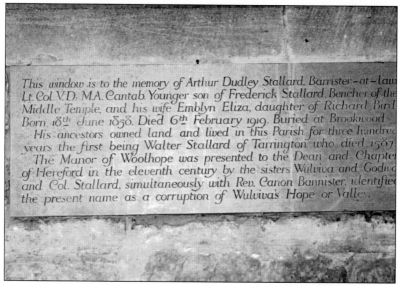

Memorial tablet with reference to Godiva window
- St George's Woolhope

extended and modified a number of times, 1310/1320, 1400s, 1736, 1748 and 1882, so none of the original structure can now be seen.

In 1848 a large buttress at the north west corner was removed. It was then that the coffin lids affixed to the north wall were found, amongst others. At the eastern end the vestry is situated. This was once part of a chapel and was formed in 1790. The chancel arch is considered to have been one of two, but when the north aisle was built, they were reduced to one.

An altar made of oak stands before a reredos made of polished marble. In the south wall a renovated 14th century piscina can be observed. Nearby stands an ancient font, which is now used to contain flowers. The altar rail posts are dated 1678. By the south door a stone vessel, which was once thought to be a stoup, is now believed to be a stone mortar of the sort found in kitchens. The nearby font with cover suspended by a counterbalance, is Victorian.

The Pub

there are two

THE BUTCHER'S ARMS

Situated on the edge of the village, this 14th century building once included a butcher's shop and abattoir. It became an ale and cider house and eventually obtained a full licence. The Butcher's has been recently refurbished, but much of the original building can be seen, with low ceiling and wooden beams. The refurbishment has been tastefully carried out and retains an old-world charm.

A patio area is positioned by a stream and there is also a garden. Bar snacks are available and there is a full menu. Overnight guests are catered for, with two letting rooms.

THE CROWN

This occupies a central position in the village next to the church and was once owned by John Jones, who was a wealthy surgeon. He donated the pub to the parish in the 1600s and it was eventually sold into private ownership. As with many of the old inns and pubs, it once brewed its own ale and had a malt house.

Over the years The Crown has been extended and altered, but has retained a lot of the original features. In the bar there is a photograph of the local Home Guard 1942-45. Some 48 men are pictured. It is interesting to note that in those days all of them had employment within the village. Among the activities, there is a Quoits League, Darts, Cricket and Football.

Bar meals or a full menu can be obtained. At the present time, overnight guests are not catered for, but preparations are in hand to enable The Crown to offer this facility.

TO CONCLUDE

On 2 July 2003 villagers at Bosbury, Herefordshire gathered to witness the marriage of Trudi Victoria Strutt and Shaun Michael Stokes. Trudi is the daughter of the vicar of Holy Trinity Church, Bosbury. Shaun is the son of the licensee of The Bell Inn, Bosbury. Truly, this is a case of 'The Village, The Church and The Pub'.

Acknowledgements

My sincere thanks to the following for their kind help, support and encourangement.

County Records, Worcester
Weston's Cider
Kelly's Directory of Worcestershire
Malvern Water (Coca-Cola Schweppes)
All named churches
All named public houses
Barbara Butcher (drawings and paintings)
Andrew Miller
Mike Izod
Malcolm Gartlands
John Fretwell
Derek Price
Joe Aspey
Ann Banks
Jeremy Ryan-Bell
Anne Hopkins

And to the many villagers who kindly aided me.

BIOGRAPHY

The author, Roy Millar was born on The Wirral, Cheshire. His connection with the area that he has written about started when he trained in the Royal Air Force Police at RAF Pershore in 1948. Upon being demobbed, he married his wife Barbara, who he met whilst at Pershore. They then lived for a short period in Cheshire.

He took up an appointment in the Insurance industry at Evesham and after a few years achieved management positions, which took him to various parts of the country, but the larger part of his career was spent in Worcestershire.

In 1985 he opted for early retirement and settled at Malvern in 1988. Always interested in history, he was able to develop his interest in churches further. It was at the suggestion of a friend that he started to write about some of the villages he had visited in the three counties of Worcestershire, Gloucestershire and Herefordshire.